The Signature Series

A journey that will last for generations to come...

Drinks on cover:

1- The Terrible Tiki
2- TNT
3- Fire & Ice
4- Honolulu Harry
5- The Flaming Bloody Deadhead
6- Butterscotch Bliss

7- The E.G.O.
8- The Magnificent Margarita
9- Berry Bonanza
10- The Rainbow
11- The WASP
12- Cookies & Cream

AuthorHouse™
1663 Liberty Drive
Bloomington, IN 47403
www.authorhouse.com
Phone: 1-800-839-8640

First published by AuthorHouse   3/22/2012

ISBN: 978-1-4670-6173-5 (sc)
ISBN: 978-1-4670-6171-1 (e)

Library of Congress Control Number: 2011960196

Printed in the United States of America

The Signature Series

A journey that will last for generations to come...

Erik G. Ossimina

authorHOUSE®

STOP

The drinks contained within this book are meant to enhance your time not ruin it. If any drink is making you feel sick, stop drinking it immediately! Drinking large amounts of alcohol quickly and in a short period of time can lead to coma or death!

Don't leave an unconscious person alone.

Consult a physician if alcohol poisoning is suspected.

Alcohol poisoning symptoms:

- Confusion
- Vomiting
- Slurred Speech
- Seizures
- Slow breathing
- Irregular breathing

- Pale skin
- Low body temperature
- Unconsciousness ("passing out")
- Dizziness
- Euphoria

If you suspect that someone has alcohol poisoning seek immediate care!   Call 911

If the person is conscious, call **800-222-1222** (in the U.S.) your call will go to your local poison control center

Calls to poison control centers are confidential

The Signature Series

A journey that will last for generations to come...

To see pictures of my drinks, merchandise & other cool things please visit me on the following sites:

www.TheSignatureSeriesbyEgo.com

Visit me on Myspace: **The Signature Series**

www.myspace.com/The-Signature-Series

Visit me on Facebook: **The Signature Series**

Check back regularly to see updates on new projects!

By Erik G. Ossimina
(E.G.O.)
2011 All Rights Reserved
Cover Concept and Design By Robin A. Ossimina

For my Wife
Kids
Family and Friends
Thanks for all the Great Times and Memories
Without you this Book Would not Have Been Written

Contents

Introduction

Welcome, I invite you to sit back, relax and get comfortable. Within the pages of this book you will find 100 of my original drink recipes. It all started in 2005 with my first drink The Jackhammer. I made this drink to be the signature drink at my private bar the Whiskey Den. I thought it would bring a different angle to my bar. Anyone who completely finished my drink would be able to sign and date the paper it was written on, which would hang on the wall of my bar. Having my drink would be a right of passage for all who would visit my bar and take part in the festivities. Another twist to signing the paper was, not only did you have to finish the entire drink but it also had to be made by someone in my bloodline. This would give more meaning to future generations to uphold and something priceless to look back on. There now was only one problem; I have three kids and only one original to pass down. My solution was to make two more drinks leaving them all with their own original wall hanging. On March 17, 2007 I completed my third drink The EGO. I was now hooked on making new and exciting drinks for my friends and family to enjoy. Everyone who tried one of my drinks would frequently ask me when I was going to create another one. It seemed to be a bigger hit than I had anticipated. It was upon completion of my fourteenth drink that I decided to come up with 100 signature drinks that I would publish for all to enjoy. The Signature Series would give people a reason to get together and celebrate no matter what the occasion. Undoubtedly one will become a new favorite of yours. For those who prefer non-alcoholic drinks there are eight drinks in the back of the book for you to try as well. So that is the story of how the Signature Series has come to be. My book has finally arrived!

Now I pass on to you the owner of this book a chance to tempt your family and friends to sign and date the pages after completion of each drink. Have some fun. Use this book to show future generations the importance of having great times with family and friends. Pass down the memories and stories that make life worth living. You can either watch life go by from the sidelines or you can throw caution to the wind and get out there and experience life with those around you. Celebrate life like you mean it.

Some of you will even have bragging rights after finishing them all. Will that be you?

Cheers!

Author Statement

This book was intended to provide those of legal drinking age a change of scenery. You should always drink in moderation and never get behind the wheel of an automobile or any other motorized equipment while enjoying my drinks or any other alcoholic beverage. Always plan ahead. Have a designated driver or plan to stay the night. Take a taxi or arrange for a ride. Remember a taxi is less expensive then a DUI. If someone has had too much to drink keep an eye on him or her. If you have to apply a little makeup and take some pictures then let it all be in fun. Remember have fun but be safe for yourself and those around you. Having said that I pass on to you the owner of this book a long and fascinating ride guaranteed to excite your senses and create an electrifying time for you, your friends and family to enjoy together.

Spirits

99 Bananas
99 Berries
Absolute Citron
Absolute Vodka
Amaretto
Apple Barrel Schnapps
Bacardi 151
Bacardi Gold Rum
Bacardi Light Rum
Baileys Irish Cream
Bartles & James Strawberry wine cooler
Beer (Budweiser)
Benedictine
Blackberry Brandy
Blue Curacao
Bombay Sapphire
Brown Crème de Cacao
Budweiser
Butterscotch Schnapps
Cabo Wabo Tequila
Captain Morgan Rum
Chambord
Champagne
Chartreuse
Cherry Jack Rum
Christian Brothers Brandy
Corazon Tequila
Crown Royal
Crystal Head Vodka
Dr. Mcgillicuddy's Cherry Schnapps
Everclear
Godiva "white chocolate liquor"
Goldschlager
Gordon's Gin
Grand Marnier
Grande Absinthe

Grape Pucker Schnapps
Green Cream De Menthe
Grey Goose Vodka
Jack Daniels
Jagermeister
Johnnie Walker Black
Jose Cuervo Tequila
Kahlua
Ketel One
Lairds Apple Jack
Malibu Rum
Midori Melon
Mike's Hard Cranberry
Mike's Hard Lemonade
Old Grand Dad
Patron XO Café
Peach Tree Schnapps
Rum
Rumple Minze
Seagram's VO Whiskey
Skyy Infusion Grape
Sloe Gin
Smirnoff Passion Fruit Twist
Smirnoff Strawberry Twist
Smirnoff Watermelon Twist
Southern Comfort
Strawberry Liqueur Leroux
Sweet Vermouth
Tangueray
Tequila
Triple Sec
Watermelon Schnapps
White Crème de Cacao
White Wine
Yago Sant Gria

Mixers

Apple Cider
Apple Juice
Bitters
Cherry Juice
Club Soda
Crushed Ice
Coco Lopez
Country Time Lemonade
Country Time Pink Lemonade
Cranberry Juice
Dry Ice
Folgers Classic Roast Coffee
Fruit Punch
Gatorade Cool Blue
Gatorade Glacier Freeze
Gatorade Rain Lime
Gatorade A.M. Orange-Strawberry
Grapefruit Juice
Grenadine
Heavy Cream
Ice

Kool Aid Cherry Flavor
Kool Aid Grape Flavor
Kool Aid Tropical Punch
Lime Juice
Lipton Iced Tea Mix
Milk
Mr. & Mrs. T "Strawberry Daiquiri
Margarita Mix"
Orange Juice
Pepsi
Pineapple Juice
Salt
Sherbet Orange
Sour Mix
Sprite
Stewarts Orange and Cream
Tea Bags
Tonic Water
Ice Cream Vanilla
Ice Cream Butterfinger
Water

*A note on the mixtures, spirits, garnishes and glassware; if for whatever reason a particular ingredient becomes unavailable simply substitute it for the closest thing available to you. Let's say that Country Time was to go out of business or is just not available where you live. Just use your favorite lemonade. Likewise I am aware that brands like Everclear are very hard to get and are even illegal in some places. Just get the closest thing you can get, start with Everclear 151. That's right Everclear comes in 151 proof. If Everclear is just not available to you, your favorite 100 proof vodka will do. If all else fails just delete the Everclear from the recipe. Remember the main reason I made this book was for everyone to have a good time. Don't let little details get in the way!

Garnishes & Other Ingredients

Apple
Banana
Blackberries
Brown Sugar
Butterscotch Syrup
Cherries (Maraschino)
Chocolate
Chocolate Syrup
Cinnamon Powder
Cinnamon Sticks
Cocktail Sticks
Crack Ups "popping Candy"
Cucumber
Grapefruit
Honey
Hot Sauce
Jell-O (blue)
Jell-O (grape)
Jell-O (green)
Jell-O (orange)
Jell-O (red)

Jell-O (yellow)
Lemons
Limes
Maple Syrup
Meal Worms
Mint Sprig
Oranges
Oreo
Peach
Pepper
Pineapple
Raspberries
Salt
Small Pepper
Straw
Strawberries
Strawberry Jelly
Sugar
Sugar Crystals Blue, Red, Orange
Whipped Cream

Glassware & Bar Tools

Bar Torch
Beater
Beer mug 16 oz.
Blender
Cheese Cloth
Clear plastic cups 8 oz.
Cocktail napkins
Cocktail Sticks or Sword
Coffee mug
Collins Glass 14 oz.
Cookie Sheet
Double Broiler
Grater
Hurricane Glass 24 oz.
Ice Cream Scooper
Ice Crusher
Knife
Ladle
Lighter
Margarita Glass 12 oz.
Martini Glass 7 oz.
Measuring Cups
Medicine Dropper

Muddler
Parchment Paper
Pens (black, blue, red, green)
Pineapple
Pint Glass 16 oz.
Pitcher (Beer)
Pitcher (Plastic)
Rocks Glass 12 oz.
Sauce Pan
Serving Plate or Platter
Shaker
Shot Glasses 1½ oz.
Skewers
Spoon
Strainer
Straws
Pilsner 23 oz.
Teapot
Tiki Mug 10 oz.
Toothpicks
Umbrellas
White Wine Glass 12oz.

The Signature Series "100"

Those who have finished all 100 Signature Drinks in this book have signed this paper and dated it, in remembrance of family, good friends, great beverages and countless memories to which these drinks were made to salute. You are among a select few who have overcome the odds. So now join me and put your name where only a few will dare to go. I salute you and I hope you had as much fun drinking them as I had creating them. Remember to follow your dreams wherever they take you. Perhaps you will take one of my tasty beverages to keep you company. Now go out and spread the word of my book to everyone you meet. You are now an ambassador of the Signature Series. Remember to always live life to it's fullest! Never give up on your dreams or your loved ones!

Sincerely, Erik G. Ossimina (E.G.O.), a.k.a. Suave

The Signature Series
"100"

The Signature Series

The Signature Series

The Signature Series

The Signature Series

The Signature Series

These are the first ten drinks to be brought to life for the Signature Series. The book is broken into ten sections with ten drinks per section. There will be two pages available to collect the signatures of those who have finished all 10 drinks from that period so there will be room for an abundance of signatures. Who can say they have had the first 10? When all 100 drinks are finished pages 12 and 13 will show the signatures of those who have dared to drink them all! Good luck & enjoy!

Others who have finished all 10 drinks on this page have signed either this paper or the next page and dated it, in remembrance of family, good friends, great beverages and countless memories to which these drinks were made to salute. So when you enjoy all of these tasty beverages do so by thinking of all the good times we share. Sincerely Erik G. Ossimina (E.G.O.), a.k.a. Suave

The Signature Series

The Jackhammer

The Jackhammer

1 ½ oz. Jack Daniels
1 ½ oz. Absolute Vodka
Pepsi
Ice
16 oz. Pint Glass
Straw
Lime

Drop ice cubes in a pint glass. Followed by the Jack Daniels and Absolute. Fill with Pepsi and stir. Add a straw and garnish with lime.

Welcome to the Signature Series, if you have a seatbelt now would be a good time to put it on. The Jackhammer has been a favorite in the Ossimina household since the early twenty-first Century. This is the first drink written down and named at my bar. The Jackhammer first appeared in 2005 after building a bar in my basement with help from my Dad. The Jackhammer came about while I was attending a wedding with my wife, her sister and their cousins. We sat together talking about the construction of my bar and the thought of having my own signature drink to serve at my private bar the Whiskey Den would be priceless. On September 24, 2005 the Jackhammer was born. Those who would finish my drink would have the honor of signing the paper that the drink recipe was printed on, which hung at my bar. So now I invite you, your friends and family to do the same here. So just remember any time you wanna get hammered, why not get Jackhammered!

Others who have finished this drink have signed either this paper or the previous page and dated it, in remembrance of family, good friends, great beverages and countless memories to which this drink was made to salute. So when you enjoy The Jackhammer do so by thinking of all the good times we share together. Sincerely Erik G. Ossimina (E.G.O.), a.k.a. Suave

The Flaming Bloody Deadhead

CAUTION
Risk
of fire

The Flaming Bloody Deadhead

1 oz. Jack Daniels

1 oz. Bacardi

1 oz. Everclear

Pineapple Juice

23 oz. Pilsner Glass

Torch or Lighter

Straw

1 oz. Southern Comfort

1 oz. Absolute Vodka

Fruit Punch

Ice

Cherry

Shaker

Spoon

Fill the glass with fruit punch about 4/5 of the way. Using a spoon float the Jack, Southern, Bacardi, Absolute then Everclear in that order on the top of the drink. This is done by turning the spoon over and slowly pouring the liquids over the spoon so it floats on the top of the liquids already in the drink. Light the drink on fire using a bar torch or lighter. Have the patron use a glass or metal object (something not flammable) to cover the glass and extinguish flame. Pour into shaker and add ice. Shake then pour back into the glass. Top with pineapple juice and a cherry. Serve with a straw.

Limit one per night!

This is the 2nd in a long list of astonishing drinks that I have invented. But beware this drink has nothing delightful about it. Don't worry you won't remember anything anyway. This is my response to the famous Long Island Iced Tea. The Long Island Iced Tea has the five white liquors including everyone's favorite Tequila. I have my own rough assortment of five liquors, which includes the hard-hitting Everclear. They bring a knife you bring a gun. That's my motto! I can see that the list of names signing this one will be few and far between. Only the tough need apply here! Since this drink is not for the faint of heart I suggest you limit this drink to one a night and for most this will be enough. A fire extinguisher should also be at the ready just in case.

Others who have finished this drink have signed either this paper or the previous page and dated it, in remembrance of family, good friends, great beverages and countless memories to which this drink was made to salute. So when you enjoy The Flaming Bloody Deadhead do so by thinking of all the good times we share together. Sincerely Erik G. Ossimina (E.G.O.), a.k.a. Suave

The E.G.O.

The E.G.O.

1½ oz. Everclear
1½ oz. Grand Marnier
Orange Juice
Ice
16 oz. Pint Glass

Cherry
Orange Slice
Umbrella and or Cocktail Sword
Cherry Juice or Grenadine
Shaker

Pour Everclear and Grand Marnier into shaker. Add ice, fill with orange juice & shake. Empty the contents of shaker into pint glass. Using the umbrella or a cocktail sword pierce the cherry & orange slice. Then put on side of glass as your garnish. Add a splash of cherry juice or Grenadine for effect.

This is the 3rd drink to be written down in this wonderful series of delightful cocktails. The E.G.O. is a sheer delight to the taste buds. Heavenly would be another way to describe your journey into this tasteful enchantment of the senses, not to mention what an ass-kicking name. Unlike the first two drinks I have created I was not the first to enjoy the taste of this drink. My beautiful wife was to have this honor. By the look on her face I could immediately tell this was a keeper. My sister was here for the unveiling of my new creation as well. Not only did she try the drink she could not stop herself and had to have another.

Others who have finished this drink have signed either this paper or the previous page and dated it, in remembrance of family, good friends, great beverages and countless memories to which this drink was made to salute. So when you enjoy The E.G.O. do so by thinking of all the good times we share together. Sincerely Erik G. Ossimina (E.G.O.), a.k.a. Suave

White Lightning

4 shots of this drink and you can sign with a Blue pen!

6 shots and you can sign with a Black pen!

8 shots and you can sign with a Green pen!

9 shots and you can sign with a Red pen!

What Color Will You Be!

White Lightning

1½ Absolute Vodka
1½ Everclear
Sprite
Ice
Shaker
1½ oz. Shot Glasses (up to 9)

Put a handful of ice into the shaker and add Everclear & Absolute. Then fill with Sprite. Have the patron of this drink shake it vigorously. When finished fill up to 9 shot glasses and enjoy.

This is the 4th drink to be written down and passed on for the enjoyment of others. With this drink I have come up with a different approach; you can enjoy 4,6,8 or 9 shots of this sinful drink and have your signature written down. With each tier of shots you finish a different color will be presented to you to sign with. Just for the record you can only sign once, so what color will you be?

4 shots of this drink and you can sign with a Blue pen!

6 shots and you can sign with a Black pen!

8 shots and you can sign with a Green pen!

9 shots and you can sign with a Red pen!

Others who have finished this drink have signed either this paper or the previous page and dated it, in remembrance of family, good friends, great beverages and countless memories to which this drink was made to salute. So when you enjoy White Lightning do so by thinking of all the good times we share together. Sincerely Erik G. Ossimina (E.G.O.), a.k.a. Suave

(Caution this drink is intended to explode and shoot out like white lightning when the unsuspecting patron shakes the shaker! So step back and enjoy. Not a drink for people without a sense of humor. Use your judgment.)

Pitcher Perfect

Drink the entire pitcher within an hour and sign your name upside down!

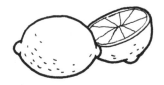

Pitcher Perfect

2 oz. Bacardi 151
2 oz. Absolute Citron
2 oz. Jack Daniels
1 oz. Tangueray
Lipton Iced Tea Mix
Water

Beer Pitcher
2-Quart Pitcher
2 Lemons
16 oz. Pint Glass
Straw
Ice

Make a batch of Lipton Iced Tea in a 2 Qt. pitcher according to directions on the container. Refrigerate until cold. Meanwhile cut 1 lemon into wedges and the second into a few lemon wheels. Make enough wedges for each pint glass and a few wheels to float in the beer pitcher. Squeeze the unused portion of lemons if any into the beer pitcher and discard. Fill beer pitcher ½ way with ice then add Bacardi, Absolute, Jack Daniels and some Tangueray for that little extra something. Fill beer pitcher with chilled iced tea. Serve in a pint glass with a straw and lemon wedge.

A snap shot of perfection comes into view at number 5. Thirsty? I hope so because signing this one can be done in one of two ways or both. The 1st way, simply fill your pint glass up and drink it down. The 2nd way is a little more time consuming. Finish the entire beer pitcher within a one-hour time limit and proudly sign your name upside down. Just turn the book upside down no need to stand on your head, unless you're into that sort of thing. I judge no one. So when life hands you lemons, take them and make the perfect pitcher of Pitcher Perfect!

<u>**Drink the entire pitcher within an hour and sign your name upside down!**</u>

Others who have finished this drink have signed either this paper or the previous page and dated it, in remembrance of family, good friends, great beverages and countless memories to which this drink was made to salute. So when you enjoy **Pitcher Perfect** do so by thinking of all the good times we share together. Sincerely Erik G. Ossimina (E.G.O.), a.k.a. Suave

Passion Fruit

Passion Fruit

Splash of Peachtree Schnapps

Splash of Apple Barrel Schnapps

Splash of Grape Pucker Schnapps

Splash of Watermelon Schnapps

Splash Absolute Vodka

Orange Juice

Cranberry Juice Shaker

Pineapple Juice

Ice

16 oz. Pint Glass

Lime

Lemon

Cherry

Umbrella

Fill pint glass halfway with ice then add a splash of peach, apple, grape and watermelon schnapps followed with a splash of vodka. Fill the remaining glass with equal parts of orange juice and cranberry juice. Pour into shaker and shake well. Pour back into pint glass and top with pineapple juice. Pierce cherry, lime and lemon with umbrella, serve on side of the glass.

This is the 6th drink in the collection. A fruity sensation will pour into your mouth when you sip on this sinfully succulent drink. Inspired by my beautiful wife, I made this drink for her to enjoy and now you too can have one as well. Sit back and enjoy the fruits of your labor with a Passion Fruit. So why not bring the Passion back into your life with a Passion Fruit! This drink tastes even better when enjoyed with that special someone.

Others who have finished this drink have signed either this paper or the previous page and dated it, in remembrance of family, good friends, great beverages and countless memories to which this drink was made to salute. So when you enjoy Passion Fruit do so by thinking of all the good times we share together. Sincerely Erik G. Ossimina (E.G.O.), a.k.a. Suave

The Patriot

"Show your true colors and sign below".

The Patriot

Grenadine
Blue Curacao
Heavy Cream
Spoon
Bar Straw or Toothpick

Hiram Walker White Crème de Cacao
Absolute Vodka
1½ oz. Shot Glass
Shaker

This is a three-layered shot. With all layers being equal in size. For the 1st layer fill 1/3 of the shot glass with Blue Curacao. For the next layer mix an equal mixture of White Crème de Cacao and heavy cream in a shaker. Using a spoon float mixture on top of the 1st layer (when using the spoon to float the mixture, turn the spoon upside down). Put shot glass in freezer until the drink hardens up. Clean shaker. Once the second layer hardens your ready for the final layer. Mix an equal mixture of vodka and Grenadine in shaker then float on top of shot. Serve with a small straw or toothpick. To enjoy shot run toothpick or straw around inside edge of shot glass to loosen cream so you can slam down shot.

The Red, White & Blue kick it off here to be my 7th magnificent drink. The red (Grenadine and vodka) the white (Crème de Cacao & heavy cream) and the blue (Blue Curacao) will help anyone feel like a real American. Patriotism has never tasted so good. This is a great drink for the 4th of July. I came up with this drink because I wanted to have a layered drink in my collection. I was trying to come up with a theme to make this drink and decided to go with a patriotic theme to salute all Americans and our friends around the world. The Red, White & Blue seemed like a great way to go! Uncle Sam says, "Show your true colors and sign below".

Others who have finished this drink have signed either this paper or the previous page and dated it, in remembrance of family, good friends, great beverages and countless memories to which this drink was made to salute. So when you enjoy The Patriot do so by thinking of all the good times we share together. Sincerely Erik G. Ossimina (E.G.O.), a.k.a. Suave

The Screaming Hungarian

The Screaming Hungarian

1½ oz. Green Crème De Menthe
1½ oz. Jagermeister
1½ oz. Everclear
Shaker
Ice
3 - 1½ oz. Shot Glasses

Fill shaker with liquor and ice. Let the shaker chill for a minute or two. Next shake and strain back into your three shot glasses. Slam the shot and enjoy!

This shot was intended to be enjoyed amongst friends. Two companions should join you on your journey. One shot for each of you. If you have to walk alone and do all three shots yourself then I applaud you. You only need to have one shot to sign. Only a real man would finish all three shots. This is the 8th drink inspired by The Screaming Viking; The Screaming Hungarian is not to be taken lightly. Many will try to go down the enlightened path but few will arrive on the other side to sign. So I invite you to walk amongst men and sign. Let it be known that if you slam it you will scream! So scream like a Hungarian!

Others who have finished this drink have signed either this paper or the previous page and dated it, in remembrance of family, good friends, great beverages and countless memories to which this drink was made to salute. So when you enjoy The Screaming Hungarian do so by thinking of all the good times we share together. Sincerely Erik G. Ossimina (E.G.O.), a.k.a. Suave

Honolulu Harry

The Original Harry

Honolulu Harry

½ oz. Everclear	Whole Pineapple	Umbrella
½ oz. Absolute Vodka	Orange	Shaker
½ oz. Bacardi	Strawberries	Spoon
½ oz. Gordon's Gin	Lemon	Lime
Splash of Strawberry Schnapps	Toothpicks	Cup
Splash of Watermelon Schnapps	Cherries	Ice
Splash of Orange Juice	Sugar	Camera
Kool Aid (Cherry Flavor)	Straw	

Cut top of pineapple off and leave on the side for later. Hollow out the inside of the pineapple and take the juices out. Strain the juice into a cup for later eliminating pulp. Put empty pineapple into freezer to chill. Clean strawberries and put them into a blender along with your juice from the pineapple. Pour the Everclear, Absolute, Bacardi and gin into the blender as well. Blend. Pour mixture back into the shaker and put into the refrigerator. Take the pineapple out. Using the pineapple as Harry's head cut up fruits to arrange his face. The patron of the drink is responsible for Harry's appearance. When finished put back into freezer to chill. Give Harry about 20 minutes to get comfortable. Take your mixture out of the refrigerator and fill with Kool Aid. Next get Harry and fill him with ice. Pour your concoction into Harry's head and add 4 to 6 tablespoons of sugar as well. There should be enough left in shaker for a refill. Stir. Then top off with the Schnapps. Stick a straw in and serve.

This is the 9th drink in the series. This one will take a little work but as in life sometimes you have to work a little harder to enjoy the finer things. This is one of those times. Honolulu Harry will bring you back to a simpler time. With him as your guide sit back, relax and put your feet up. You'll feel like your sitting at a beach in Hawaii taking in some rays. One more element to this majestic cocktail is that you get to design his appearance. Feel free to use whatever you want to construct his face. You should also have your camera ready to take your picture with your new friend. Be creative and make me proud! Send me a picture of you and your new friend and I might put you on one of my web pages for all to see.

Others who have finished this drink have signed either this paper or the previous page and dated it, in remembrance of family, good friends, great beverages and countless memories to which this drink was made to salute. So when you enjoy Honolulu Harry do so by thinking of all the good times we share together. Sincerely Erik G. Ossimina (E.G.O.), a.k.a. Suave

The Rainbow

The Rainbow

¼ Cup Midori Melon	Green Jell-O
¼ Cup Everclear	Yellow Jell-O
¼ Cup Absolute Vodka	Red Jell-O
¼ Cup Grand Marnier	Orange Jell-O
¼ Cup Bombay Sapphire	Blue Jell-O
¼ Cup Grape Pucker	Grape Jell-O
8 oz. Clear Plastic Cups	Water

The liquor above goes with the Jell-O listed to the right of it. Start with the green then yellow, red, orange, blue and finally top with purple. Use a whole packet of Jell-O for each layer and one cup of hot water, ¾ cup of cold water and ¼ cup of liquor. Do one color at a time. Before adding the next layer make sure the previous layer has cooled.

Jell-O anyone? This is the ultimate in jell-o shots. A little time consuming but The Rainbow is well worth the wait. This massive shot of happiness is the 10th drink in the series. You'll find a pot of gold after every layer. The colors of the rainbow wait to show you true pleasure and tranquility. A great way to spice up any party, The Rainbow will unquestionably be the right hand man for any host who wants to have a celebration to remember! On page 216 The Iridescent Rainbow is tailor made for the ladies, lighter and prettier. Go to page 238 and make a non-alcoholic one for the kids. They are great to make at parties, but may I suggest that you either make the alcoholic versions or the non-alcoholic version there is a chance that they could get mixed up.

Others who have finished this drink have signed either this paper or the previous page and dated it, in remembrance of family, good friends, great beverages and countless memories to which this drink was made to salute. So when you enjoy The Rainbow do so by thinking of all the good times we share together. Sincerely Erik G. Ossimina (E.G.O.), a.k.a. Suave

The Signature Series

Others who have finished all 10 drinks on this page have signed either this paper or the next page and dated it, in remembrance of family, good friends, great beverages and countless memories to which these drinks were made to salute. So when you enjoy all of these tasty beverages do so by thinking of all the good times we share. Sincerely Erik G. Ossimina (E.G.O.), a.k.a. Suave

The Signature Series

The Lucky Leprechaun

The Lucky Leprechaun

1 oz. Absolute Vodka
1 oz. Midori Melon
Green Crème De Menthe
6 oz. Sprite
Lime
6 - 1½ oz. Shot Glasses
Shaker
Dice
Ice

Run a lime wedge around the rim of the shot glasses and discard. Pour the Absolute & Midori into the shaker and add ice. Add Sprite then strain into shot glasses. Top each shot off with a splash of Green Crème De Menthe for good luck. Makes enough for 6 shots.

The Lucky Leprechaun will tell you on a scale of 1 – 6 just how lucky you really are. Roll 1 die to see how many shots you need to drink in order to sign. Let's see if the luck of the Irish is with you on this one, my 11th creation. Will it be 6 or maybe just 2 shots, there's only one-way to find out. Catch this one and a pot of gold might not be there, but your signature will. Always great on St. Patrick's Day to go along with your green beer. The Lucky Leprechaun will be a good luck charm for you. When signing this one put the number of shots you drank next to your signature.

Others who have finished this drink have signed either this paper or the previous page and dated it, in remembrance of family, good friends, great beverages and countless memories to which this drink was made to salute. So when you enjoy The Lucky Leprechaun do so by thinking of all the good times we share together. Sincerely Erik G. Ossimina (E.G.O.), a.k.a. Suave

Twisted

2 oz. Absolute Vodka
2 oz. Butterscotch Schnapps
2 oz. Bailey's Irish Cream
½ Cup Milk
3 Scoops Butterfinger Ice Cream
3 Cups Crushed Ice
Chocolate Syrup
Butterscotch Syrup
Whipped Cream
24 oz. Hurricane Glass
Ice Crusher
Blender
Straw

Crush ice using the ice crusher then put in blender with milk, alcohol and ice cream. Blend till mixture is smooth. Drizzle chocolate and butterscotch syrup in the hurricane glass. Then fill glass with the mixture from the blender. Spray whipped cream on top of glass and drizzle the syrups on top. Serve with a straw.

This is the 12th drink to come down the pike. Appetizing and full of flavor, Twisted will turn your taste buds inside out and upside down. The bigger the straw the easier time you will have putting this one away. So twist one up today! I enjoyed this drink for the first time on the 20th of April 2010. I keep coming back for more, you will too!

Others who have finished this drink have signed either this paper or the previous page and dated it, in remembrance of family, good friends, great beverages and countless memories to which this drink was made to salute. So when you enjoy Twisted do so by thinking of all the good times we share together. Sincerely Erik G. Ossimina (E.G.O.), a.k.a. Suave

The Inferno

The Inferno

1 oz. Tequila
8 oz. Orange Juice
Grenadine
12 oz. Rocks Glass
Umbrella

1 oz. Everclear
Hot Sauce
Small Hot Pepper
Shaker

Pour Tequila & ¾ oz. of Everclear and orange juice to fill rocks glass into shaker (shake). Line the rim of your rocks glass with hot sauce, then empty shaker into the rocks glass. Top drink with ¼ oz. of Everclear and add a few drops of grenadine for effect. Light the cocktail on fire. Extinguish the flame after drink has heated up 10-15 seconds. Using your umbrella stab a small pepper (if available, if you don't have pepper the umbrella is unnecessary). Put garnish on side of glass. (No straws for this drink!)

How you feeling HOT HOT HOT!!! You will be after tasting this concoction. This is the 13th drink in this chain of incredible cocktails. This drink will test the fortitude of any man (or woman for that matter) who dare tempt fate and swallow this. So I welcome you to come on and taste The Inferno for yourself, you might be surprised. No straws in this one! Knock it back & sign below! As with the Flaming Bloody Deadhead an extinguisher should always be at the ready! My good friend Scott Ferguson was the first one on line to sign this one on December 22, 2007 after already slamming down the E.G.O. Now don't let Scott show you up! Put your John Hancock down and show Scott he's not special, well in a good way anyway! Presently he is in a metal band called Stagger from the Jersey Shore. If you run into him extend your finger & let him know that he's #1.

Others who have finished this drink have signed either this paper or the previous page and dated it, in remembrance of family, good friends, great beverages and countless memories to which this drink was made to salute. So when you enjoy The Inferno do so by thinking of all the good times we share together. Sincerely Erik G. Ossimina (E.G.O.), a.k.a. Suave

CAUTION
Risk
of fire

The Zebra

The Zebra

2/3 Shot Brown Crème de Cocoa
1/3 Shot White Crème de Cocoa
Heavy cream
1 ½ oz. Shot glass
Spoon
2 Shakers
Chocolate Syrup
Bar straw
Whipped Cream

This is a three-layered shot. With all layers being equal in size. For the 1st layer mix in a shaker Brown Crème de Cocoa and a splash of chocolate syrup. Make enough for 2 layers. Pour half of the mixture into shot glass. Now for the second layer mix an equal portion of heavy cream and White Crème de Cocoa in a shaker. Using a spoon float mixture on top of 1st layer (when using the spoon to float the mixture, turn the spoon upside down). Put shot glass in freezer until the drink hardens up. Once the second layer hardens you're ready for the final layer. Float remaining mixture in the shaker from 1st layer on top of shot for the final layer. ** Spray a small amount of whipped cream on top of shot and drizzle a little chocolate syrup. Serve with a small straw or toothpick. To enjoy shot run toothpick or straw around inside edge of shot glass to loosen cream so you can slam down shot.

Coming in at #14. Once named after everyone's favorite cookie, The Zebra is it's new name. No need to have any problems with cookie people you know how they can be. But what you call it in the privacy of your home is your business. So it seems like there is no end to the insanity of mouth-watering drinks I will create. It was back in 2008 when I created this drink that I decided to come up with a 100 signature drinks to publish for all to enjoy!

*** I added this when I changed it to the Zebra.*

Others who have finished this drink have signed either this paper or the previous page and dated it, in remembrance of family, good friends, great beverages and countless memories to which this drink was made to salute. So when you enjoy a Zebra do so by thinking of all the good times we share together. Sincerely Erik G. Ossimina (E.G.O.), a.k.a. Suave

Peppermint Patty

Peppermint Patty

1 ½ oz. Rumple Minze
1 ½ oz. Midori Melon
3 oz. Sprite
4 - 1½ oz. Shot Glasses
Shaker
Spoon
Ice

Pour Rumple Minze and ice into the shaker, followed by Sprite. Let chill. Next pour equal amounts into each of the 4 shot glasses. Finally use a spoon and float the Midori on top of your shots.

Congratulations! you have made it to the 15th drink & on your way to a hundred. That's if you're going in order. Who has had all 15 to this point? I bet not many! You only need to finish 2 shots to sign this one; so find a friend and get cracking!

Others who have finished this drink have signed either this paper or the previous page and dated it, in remembrance of family, good friends, great beverages and countless memories to which this drink was made to salute. So when you enjoy Peppermint Patty do so by thinking of all the good times we share together. Sincerely Erik G. Ossimina (E.G.O.), a.k.a. Suave

Blue Light Special

Blue Light Special

3 oz. Blue Curacao
3 oz. Absolute Vodka
3 Cups Cool Blue Gatorade
3 Cups Crushed Ice
24 oz. Hurricane Glass
Ice Crusher
Whipped Cream
Blue sugar Crystals
Blender
Straw

Fill hurricane glass with crushed ice. Blend alcohol with Gatorade. Then fill glass with mixture from blender. Spray Whipped Cream on top of drink and cover with blue sugar crystals. Serve with a straw.

Attention shoppers today's Blue Light Special comes to you as # 16 in the aisle of great taste. The color blue has never tasted so good.

Others who have finished this drink have signed either this paper or the previous page and dated it, in remembrance of family, good friends, great beverages and countless memories to which this drink was made to salute. So when you enjoy a Blue Light Special do so by thinking of all the good times we share together. Sincerely Erik G. Ossimina (E.G.O.), a.k.a. Suave

Coco Loco

Coco Loco

2 oz. Malibu Rum
½ oz. Everclear
½ oz. Tequila
Orange Juice
Pineapple Juice
Cranberry Juice
Orange Wheel

Lime Wheel
Salt
Shaker
16 oz. Pint Glass
Straw
Ice

Pour Malibu, Everclear and Tequila into your shaker. Add equal portions of orange, pineapple and cranberry juice. Shake. Run lime around rim of pint glass and coat with salt. Fill glass halfway with ice. Pour shaker into glass and enjoy with orange and lime wheel as your garnish. Serve with a straw.

This is the 17th drink I have created to ensure a happier world in which to live in. "He has done it again" raved all that have enjoyed this one so far. Bartenders should be prepared; those around you will likely be ordering more before they have even finished their first one. One at a time folks, there's plenty to go around. Be sure to keep a close eye on your ingredients; you don't want to run out!

Others who have finished this drink have signed either this paper or the previous page and dated it, in remembrance of family, good friends, great beverages and countless memories to which this drink was made to salute. So when you enjoy Coco Loco do so by thinking of all the good times we share together. Sincerely Erik G. Ossimina (E.G.O.), a.k.a. Suave

Blackout

THIS'LL GRAB YA!

Blackout

1 ½ oz Jack Daniels
½ oz. Absolute
½ oz. Everclear
Pepsi
16 oz. Pint Glass
Ice
Lime Wheel
Straw

Fill glass halfway with ice and then add the Jack Daniels, Absolute & Everclear. Fill glass with Pepsi. Put lime wheel on edge of glass as garnish. Serve with a straw.

The Blackout was originally the 3rd drink but was put on the back burner and is now ready as the 18th drink. The Blackout will allow you to become one with your inner self. (Not to be digested while driving, using heavy equipment, hazardous machinery or just simply walking around.) So if you have nothing to do for the next day or two, I tempt you to experience a Blackout. I suggest you write down the date before drinking it cause you just might not remember it when it comes time to sign!

Others who have finished this drink have signed either this paper or the previous page and dated it, in remembrance of family, good friends, great beverages and countless memories to which this drink was made to salute. So when you enjoy a Blackout do so by thinking of all the good times we share together. Sincerely Erik G. Ossimina (E.G.O.), a.k.a. Suave

The Atomic Punch

The Atomic Punch

1¾ oz. Southern Comfort
1¾ oz. Absolute Vodka
Kool Aid (Cherry Flavor)
Crack Ups (popping candy)
16 oz. Pint Glass
Ice

Pour Southern Comfort and Absolute into the pint glass, fill with ice then add Kool Aid. Empty a packet of Crack Ups into the drink and serve.

Tasty is one way to describe my 19ᵗʰ drink, another way would be and I quote " Oh God, Oh my God. I don't think you should drink that." Said my stunning wife after tasting the Atomic Punch. In all fairness she didn't have the crack ups when she tried it. I think I'll have to make it for her again. Your tongue will tingle with excitement after every sip. No need for a straw here. Taste the explosion that is an Atomic Punch!

Others who have finished this drink have signed either this paper or the previous page and dated it, in remembrance of family, good friends, great beverages and countless memories to which this drink was made to salute. So when you enjoy The Atomic Punch do so by thinking of all the good times we share together. Sincerely Erik G. Ossimina (E.G.O.), a.k.a. Suave

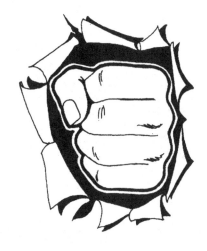

The WASP

The Wasp

1 oz. Whiskey VO
1 oz. Absolute Vodka
1 oz. Southern Comfort
    Pepsi

Ice
Lime
Lemon
16 oz. Pint Glass
Straw

Pour the Whiskey, Absolute & Southern Comfort into the pint glass. Add ice, fill with Pepsi. Garnish with lemon & lime wedges. Serve with a straw.

The Wasp is my 20th drink, which was inspired by the music of The Doors. It just came to me as I sat there pondering life. If you ask me, I think that when you enjoy the Wasp maybe you should throw the Doors on, sit back and enjoy their music. The Wasp will delight your tongue in ways it has never tasted before. Take this for an example: I was sick with a sore throat and basically not feeling well but after devouring this magical potion everything came into view and I instantly felt better. I'm not saying that this miracle of a drink cures a cold but I'm not saying it doesn't either! So I say why not try one, what do you have to lose besides a cold. I think it might just keep you from getting ill in the first place. So drink up, get stung and sign!

Others who have finished this drink have signed either this paper or the previous page and dated it, in remembrance of family, good friends, great beverages and countless memories to which this drink was made to salute. So when you enjoy The Wasp do so by thinking of all the good times we share together. Sincerely Erik G. Ossimina (E.G.O.), a.k.a. Suave

The Signature Series

Others who have finished all 10 drinks on this page have signed either this paper or the next page and dated it, in remembrance of family, good friends, great beverages and countless memories to which these drinks were made to salute. So when you enjoy all of these tasty beverages do so by thinking of all the good times we share. Sincerely Erik G. Ossimina (E.G.O.), a.k.a. Suave

The Signature Series

The Rocking Robin
&
The R.A.O.

The R.A.O.
&
The Rocking Robin

1 ½ Captain Morgan / Favorite Rum
1 ½ Absolute Vodka
16 oz. Pint Glass
Orange Juice
Umbrella

6 – 1 ½ oz. Shot Glasses
Cherries
Straw
Ice

The RAO:

Pour Captain Morgan and Absolute into pint glass. Add ice and fill with orange juice. Stir. Garnish with 3 cherries, umbrella and a straw.

The Rocking Robin:

Pour your favorite rum along with Absolute, orange juice and ice into the shaker. Shake. Strain the shaker into the shot glasses. Put a cherry into every other shot glass. Slam shots!

The 21st and 22nd drinks are named after my wonderful sister. The Rocking Robin & The R.A.O. are two different drinks all together. Hence there are two different recipes, one for each. Sounds logical to me, have two drinks have two different recipes right? I'll just put them on the same page. The first way is known as The R.A.O. It would consist of using Captain Morgan as the rum the way my sister would enjoy. The Rocking Robin uses any other rum that you would prefer to enjoy. My personal favorite would be Bacardi but here you choose your poison. I made this one with 6 shots. One for each year I have on her. You have to drink all 6 shots to sign. Remember that you can sign this paper twice, once for each drink. A red pen will be used to sign when you enjoy the Rocking Robin any other color for the R.A.O. Do tell which rum you might be enjoying. I am sure everybody would like to know. My sister's only request is that her drinks be served with 3 cherries. Why not, whatever makes you happy I always say. I'll bet that if you enjoy one or even both of these scrumptious beverages you'll be happy too. So dive in and let's all get a little happy☺!

Others who have finished this drink have signed either this paper or the previous page and dated it, in remembrance of family, good friends, great beverages and countless memories to which this drink was made to salute. So when you enjoy a Rocking Robin and/or a R.A.O. do so by thinking of all the good times we share together. Sincerely Erik G. Ossimina (E.G.O.), a.k.a. Suave

Hardcore Sangria

Hardcore Sangria

Yago Sant' Gria'
2 oz. Christian Brothers Brandy
2 oz. Absolute Vodka
2 oz. Southern Comfort
1 cup Tonic Water
½ Cup Water
½ Cup Sugar
Ice

Strawberries
Cherries
2 Lemons
2 Limes
2 Orange
24 oz. Hurricane Glasses
Glass Pitcher
Skewers

Put ½ cup of sugar & ½ cup of water in a saucepan and bring to a boil. Stirring occasionally until sugar dissolves. Remove from heat and let cool for half an hour. Meanwhile take a lemon, lime and orange along with some strawberries and cherries. Squeeze the juices and pour into your saucepan. Discard fruit. Fill pitcher with ice and add the liquor. Pour your ingredients from the saucepan into the pitcher. Next add 1 cup of chilled tonic water and fill with Yago Sant' Gria'. Stir. Finally slice remaining fruit in wedges and stab with skewers. Put loaded skewers into each hurricane glass along with ice. Finally your ready to fill the hurricane glasses; add a straw and umbrella. Extra skewers should be placed in the glass pitcher for the next glass.

A tasty treat checks in at spot #23. Hardcore Sangria is a drink for wine lovers everywhere! This drink left my in-laws wanting more and my wife flush in the face, not to mention she had to sit down after only a few sips. They all know a good thing when they see one, hope you do too. The intoxicating aroma of this insane drink will drive you crazy and wanting more. Obey your needs and dive in. My Hardcore Sangria serves about 4 people, or 1 really thirsty person. But don't delay, it will not last long so get it while the getting's good.

Others who have finished this drink have signed either this paper or the previous page and dated it, in remembrance of family, good friends, great beverages and countless memories to which this drink was made to salute. So when you enjoy Hardcore Sangria do so by thinking of all the good times we share together. Sincerely Erik G. Ossimina (E.G.O.), a.k.a. Suave

Ossimina's Hot & Hard Spiced Cider

Ossimina's Hot & Hard Spiced Cider

8 oz. Apple Cider
1 ½ oz. Laird's Apple Jack
1 oz. Absolute Vodka
1/3-Cup Brown Sugar
Cinnamon Sticks
Saucepan

Apple
Orange
Coffee Mug
Cheesecloth
String

Cut apples and oranges into thin slices. Put them into the cheesecloth. Add some cinnamon sticks and tie up cloth with a string. In a saucepan add 8 oz.'s of cider per person and brown sugar. Put cheesecloth in the saucepan and bring to a boil. Reduce heat, cover and let simmer for 10 minutes. Dispense 1 ½ oz of Laird's Apple Jack & 1 oz. Absolute Vodka into each mug. Discard cheesecloth and pour contents of saucepan into the coffee mugs. Garnish with cinnamon stick, stir and serve.

This is a drink that will wake up your taste buds. My 24th drink is the perfect way to start your day. Picture this; you wake up to the smell of warmed apple cider on a chilly morning to have a loved one surprise you with some tasty hot-spiced cider. You both sit outside listening to nature as you take a swig from your mug and think how wonderful life can be with the right atmosphere. My mug of cider is even more delightful after a hard morning of shoveling snow. Some say it will relieve your back pain after such laborious activities. So get on the fast track to feeling good physically and mentally by sipping down this tasty treat. Great for the kids after being out in the snow all day, of course you would not put the alcohol in their mugs. It's a drink that the whole family can enjoy together. So whether you're having a snowball fight or just lying around, nothing beats Ossimina's Hot and Hard Spiced Cider on a chilly morning!

Others who have finished this drink have signed either this paper or the previous page and dated it, in remembrance of family, good friends, great beverages and countless memories to which this drink was made to salute. So when you enjoy Ossimina's Hot & Hard Spiced Cider do so by thinking of all the good times we share together. Sincerely Erik G. Ossimina (E.G.O.), a.k.a. Suave

<u>Tropical Breeze</u>

Tropical Breeze

1 ½ oz. Absolute Vodka
Grapefruit Juice
Orange Juice
Country Time Pink Lemonade
Ice
16 oz. Pint Glass
Shaker

In a shaker pour equal portions of grapefruit juice, orange juice and Country Time Pink Lemonade. Add Absolute and ice, shake. Pour into the pint glass and serve with a straw.

Where am I? Is this heaven? I think so! In the company of family and friends enjoying a delicious beverage. What could be better then that on a summer's afternoon? You are a quarter of the way there. My 25th drink will not leave you high and dry but will amuse your senses as you drift off into a summers dream!

Others who have finished this drink have signed either this paper or the previous page and dated it, in remembrance of family, good friends, great beverages and countless memories to which this drink was made to salute. So when you enjoy a Tropical Breeze do so by thinking of all the good times we share together. Sincerely Erik G. Ossimina (E.G.O.), a.k.a. Suave

Cherry Bomb

Cherry Bomb

Maraschino Stemmed Cherries
Bailey's Irish Cream
Chocolate (Melting Chocolate)
Medicine Dropper
Double Boiler
Beater

Serving Plate or Platter
Parchment Paper
Cookie Sheet
Chocolate Syrup
Knife

Melt chocolate in a double boiler. Next dip (dry) cherries into chocolate and place on a cookie sheet lined with parchment paper. Let cool. When chocolate has hardened cut a small hole on the top of the cherry with a knife. Then using the end of the beater punch a hole into the cherry. (I find the small end of the beater makes a great puncture hole in the cherry; you can use anything handy to make the hole a little larger for the alcohol to sit in). Fill medicine dropper with Bailey's Irish Cream and inject into the top of cherries. Refrigerate cherries till chocolate hardens. Before serving cherries, top off the cherries one more time with the Bailey's Irish Cream. Place finished cherries on the serving plate or platter then drizzle chocolate syrup over then in a fancy manor and serve.

In 26th place comes the Cherry Bomb. Great at parties, serve on a platter and let your guests indulge in this delicious treat. One, two, three how many will you have? Simple to make and fun to eat, what more could you ask for?

Others who have finished this drink have signed either this paper or the previous page and dated it, in remembrance of family, good friends, great beverages and countless memories to which this drink was made to salute. So when you enjoy a Cherry Bomb do so by thinking of all the good times we share together. Sincerely Erik G. Ossimina (E.G.O.), a.k.a. Suave

A Sugared Strawberry

A Sugared Strawberry

Strawberry
Sugar
Leroux Strawberry Liqueur
Serving Plate or Platter
Shot Glass
Knife

Cut the top off a strawberry and hollow it out carefully not damaging the sides of the strawberry. Rinse strawberries off. Next roll strawberry around in a bowl of sugar. Pour the Leroux Strawberry Liqueur into the strawberry and place strawberry in the shot glass and serve.

Another simple and tasty treat in the tradition of the Cherry Bomb, the Sugared Strawberry will not disappoint. You might want to have a napkin near by when enjoying this luscious treat. Have someone lick off the tasty residue you left behind. This could be a treat for the both of you! You're welcome! Either way I hope you enjoy them. The Sugared Strawberry comes in at number 27. Make a whole bunch to serve on a platter for your next party and watch them disappear as the number of names that appear here multiply!

Others who have finished this drink have signed either this paper or the previous page and dated it, in remembrance of family, good friends, great beverages and countless memories to which this drink was made to salute. So when you enjoy a Sugared Strawberry do so by thinking of all the good times we share together. Sincerely Erik G. Ossimina (E.G.O.), a.k.a. Suave

The Cyclone

The Cyclone

1 ½ oz. Everclear
1 oz. Absolute Vodka
1 oz. Smirnoff's Watermelon Twist
Grapefruit Juice
Orange Juice
Country Time Pink Lemonade
Ice
16 oz. Pint Glass
Shaker
Straw
Cherry

Pour your liquor into the pint glass. Then add equal parts of grapefruit juice, orange juice and pink lemonade. Pour into shaker. Drop in a cherry. Shake vigorously. Then pour back into the pint glass. Add ice and serve with a straw.

The 28th drink comes in as a whirlwind. This drink will pick you up and throw you for a loop if you're not careful. But I say throw caution to the wind and drink it up. Enjoy the cherry after you finish your drink.

Others who have finished this drink have signed either this paper or the previous page and dated it, in remembrance of family, good friends, great beverages and countless memories to which this drink was made to salute. So when you enjoy a Cyclone do so by thinking of all the good times we share together. Sincerely Erik G. Ossimina (E.G.O.), a.k.a. Suave

Apple Of My Eye

Apple Of My Eye

1 oz. Laird's Apple Jack
1 oz. Apple Barrel Schnapps
Apple Juice
Apple Slice
12 oz. Rocks Glass
Ice

Put a handful of ice into the rocks glass and add the Apple Jack & Apple Barrel.
Fill with apple juice. Add an apple slice for garnish.

Apple Of My Eye is lucky number 29. I think this is a great drink to sip down while enjoying a meal instead of a glass of wine. It will bring out the flavor in your feasts and spread a magical atmosphere at the dinner table for all who accompany you to enjoy.

Others who have finished this drink have signed either this paper or the previous page and dated it, in remembrance of family, good friends, great beverages and countless memories to which this drink was made to salute. So when you enjoy Apple Of My Eye do so by thinking of all the good times we share together. Sincerely Erik G. Ossimina (E.G.O.), a.k.a. Suave

Manhattan On Bourbon Street

Manhattan On Bourbon Street

1 ½ Seagram's VO Whiskey
1 ½ Jack Daniels
½ Sweet Vermouth
Cherry
7 oz. Martini Glass
Shaker
Strainer
Ice

Put ice and liquor into the shaker. Let stand for a minute or two then strain into glass. Garnish with a cherry.

Number 30 is here so hold on to your buds, taste buds that is. My dad was to be the first to try this one out. I knew if he enjoyed it, it would be a keeper. He did so here it is. Why not join my dad and slam one down. Who knows maybe this will be your new drink. Well, I poured one of these delightful drinks for myself and my wife came over and decided that she would try this one herself. And I quote, "everything went warm." I had made this drink for my Dads enjoyment but who would have thought that my wife would be signing this one. It's like me eating a salad instead of a steak. This might end up as one of my wife's new favorite drinks. She did slip in and out of consciousness while downing this one. But in the end she stayed right with me and said that she would drink it again! I believe that she has just called everyone out!

Others who have finished this drink have signed either this paper or the previous page and dated it, in remembrance of family, good friends, great beverages and countless memories to which this drink was made to salute. So when you enjoy Manhattan On Bourbon Street do so by thinking of all the good times we share together. Sincerely Erik G. Ossimina (E.G.O.), a.k.a. Suave

The Signature Series

Others who have finished all 10 drinks on this page have signed either this paper or the next page and dated it, in remembrance of family, good friends, great beverages and countless memories to which these drinks were made to salute. So when you enjoy all of these tasty beverages do so by thinking of all the good times we share. Sincerely Erik G. Ossimina (E.G.O.), a.k.a. Suave

The Signature Series

Tequila Time Bomb

Tequila Time Bomb

1 oz. Jose Cuervo Tequila
1 oz. Corazon Tequila
¾ oz. Everclear
¾ oz. Crown Royal
Orange Juice
Cranberry Juice
16 oz. Pint Glass
Shaker
Ice

Fill shaker with ice, liquor and equal amounts of orange juice and cranberry juice. Shake, Shake, Shake; Shake, Shake, Shake; Shake your Shaker, Shake your Shaker! Fill pint glass with ice and dispense shaker into pint glass.

It's only a matter of time until this one explodes in your mouth! The Tequila Time Bomb is here so sit down and get comfortable. Will you be able to defuse this one or will it detonate? I encourage you to take a chance and see what you're made of, possibly literally. This is the 31st drink; and furthermore I have made this one for my wife's delightful sister Lisa. Because with out her persistence this drink might not have been made. Her passion for tequila has made me bring to you a sure classic. So thank you Lisa! I hope you all enjoy this one as well! Now this is spooky, upon finishing the drink and getting ready to print it out "Tequila Sunrise" by the Eagles started playing on my radio! This drink was meant to be!

Others who have finished this drink have signed either this paper or the previous page and dated it, in remembrance of family, good friends, great beverages and countless memories to which this drink was made to salute. So when you enjoy a Tequila Time Bomb do so by thinking of all the good times we share together. Sincerely Erik G. Ossimina (E.G.O.), a.k.a. Suave

The Devil's Dream

The Devil's Dream

1 oz. Jack Daniels
1 oz. Southern Comfort
1 Beer (Budweiser Preferred)
16 oz. Beer Mug

Dispense Jack Daniels into beer mug along with the Southern Comfort. Pour beer directly into mug allowing for some foam. Don't stir.

If the Devil dared to dream this is what he would have on his mind. Number 32 will wake you up after a hard days work. So sit back and enjoy, everything will work out in the end; but it might just cost you your soul. Be warned! The Devil's Dream to be made properly should be made with The King of Beers but if you must use a sub par beer than that's your decision. I will not get offended.

Others who have finished this drink have signed either this paper or the previous page and dated it, in remembrance of family, good friends, great beverages and countless memories to which this drink was made to salute. So when you enjoy The Devil's Dream do so by thinking of all the good times we share together. Sincerely Erik G. Ossimina (E.G.O.), a.k.a. Suave

Landslide

Landslide

1 ½ oz. Bailey's Irish Cream
1 oz. Kahlua
1 oz. Absolute Vodka
1 oz. Dark Crème De Cacao
Chocolate Syrup
Whipped Cream
16 oz. Beer Mug
Shaker
Straw
Milk
Ice

Put some ice cubes into a shaker, add liquor and fill with milk. Shake it good. Twirl chocolate syrup along the inside of the beer mug. Pour contents of shaker into the mug. Spray whipped cream on top and drizzle chocolate syrup on top of whipped cream. Serve with a straw.

The Landslide comes to us as number 33. One of my wife's favorite drinks is the Mudslide. So I figured instead of the mundane Mudslide perhaps she would prefer something superior for her taste buds to enjoy. I could tell after her first sip that I had succeeded in bringing to life another perfect recipe. My lovely wife loved the taste of this drink so much she felt obligated to say a few words. " Of all the delicious drinks my very handsome husband has created this is by far my favorite. He knows what to make for me when he is in trouble, luckily for me that is often ☺." We both hope you enjoy this one. I guarantee 100 % satisfaction on this one. (If you don't like it tell someone who cares! Haha!)

Others who have finished this drink have signed either this paper or the previous page and dated it, in remembrance of family, good friends, great beverages and countless memories to which this drink was made to salute. So when you enjoy a Landslide do so by thinking of all the good times we share together. Sincerely Erik G. Ossimina (E.G.O.), a.k.a. Suave

The Train

The Train

½ oz. Absolute Vodka

½ oz. Chambord

½ oz. Southern Comfort

½ oz. Triple Sec

½ oz. Kahlua

Beer (Budweiser)

Sprite

Sprite

Cranberry Juice

Orange Juice

½ oz. Bailey's Irish Cream

5 - 1½ Shot Glasses

The train consists of 5 shots and 1 beer. 1st shot is Absolute and Sprite, 2nd Chambord and Sprite, 3rd Southern Comfort and cranberry juice, the 4th Triple Sec and orange juice, finally the 5th Kahlua and Bailey's Irish Cream. Shots to be done in a row and finished with a beer.

C'mon and ride my train. Drink the five shots in a row and finish with a beer, preferably a Budweiser but you can choose which beer you like. Use your beer as a brake and slow the train down if need be. You have a choice, will your train be on the local track or the express? For those of you who choose the express let everybody scream chug, a chug, a chug, a chug, a chug, choo choo, while you slam these 5 shots down. Let me tell you, you'll be loaded like a freight train after sampling this one. After finishing the five shots right in a row slow that train down with a beer of your choice. The Train comes into the station at number 34 for those of you who are keeping track. I would like to advise all riders to keep their hands in the train at all times and please no flash photography while the train is in motion.

Others who have finished this drink have signed either this paper or the previous page and dated it, in remembrance of family, good friends, great beverages and countless memories to which this drink was made to salute. So when you enjoy The Train do so by thinking of all the good times we share together. Sincerely Erik G. Ossimina (E.G.O.), a.k.a. Suave

Lumber Jack

Lumber Jack

1 oz. Jack Daniels
Log Cabin Maple Syrup
1 ½ oz. Shot Glass
Shaker
Ice

Pour Jack Daniels into shaker loaded with ice and add a drop of maple syrup. Shake. Next run syrup around edge of shot glass. Once shaker has chilled, empty into shot glass and top off with another drop of syrup.

The Lumber Jack saws in at number 35. A few of these will go a long way especially after chopping wood all day. So put on your flannel, sharpen your axe and tie up your boots. It's time to chop down some trees and do some shots. Make Paul Bunyan proud!

Others who have finished this drink have signed either this paper or the previous page and dated it, in remembrance of family, good friends, great beverages and countless memories to which this drink was made to salute. So when you enjoy a Lumber Jack do so by thinking of all the good times we share together. Sincerely Erik G. Ossimina (E.G.O.), a.k.a. Suave

Black Jack

Black Jack

1 ¾ oz. Johnny Walker Black Label
1 ¾ oz. Jack Daniels
Pepsi
16 oz. Pint Glass
Straw
Ice
Cherry
Lime Wheel
Cocktail Sword

Pour Johnny & Jack into a pint glass, add ice then fill with Pepsi. For the garnish stab cherry and lime with cocktail sword and hang on edge of glass.

A distant cousin of the original Jack Hammer, the Black Jack has a style & taste all it's own. If flavor and tranquility are what you crave then the Black Jack is what you require. This drink is your ace in the hole. The Black Jack is a fine companion to have with you when visiting the tables in Atlantic City or just playing cards at home. You'll be saying hit me again or perhaps you'll just double down with my 36th drink.

Others who have finished this drink have signed either this paper or the previous page and dated it, in remembrance of family, good friends, great beverages and countless memories to which this drink was made to salute. So when you enjoy a Blackjack do so by thinking of all the good times we share together. Sincerely Erik G. Ossimina (E.G.O.), a.k.a. Suave

Mystic Blue

Mystic Blue

1 oz. Blue Curacao
1 oz. Bombay Sapphire
Sprite
12 oz. Rocks Glass
2 Bar Straws
Ice

Fill rocks glass ½ way with ice then pour Blue Curacao and Bombay Sapphire in. Fill with Sprite, stir and serve with 2 bar straws.

Spiritual refreshment for your soul, Mystic Blue will quench your thirst with its supernatural powers restoring your balance with nature. At number 37 Mystic Blue's power s of contentment will satisfy all who devour it. A great drink to have while meditating and being one with yourself. Mystic Blue is the drink for you!

Others who have finished this drink have signed either this paper or the previous page and dated it, in remembrance of family, good friends, great beverages and countless memories to which this drink was made to salute. So when you enjoy Mystic Blue do so by thinking of all the good times we share together. Sincerely Erik G. Ossimina (E.G.O.), a.k.a. Suave

Strawberry Kiss

Strawberry Kiss

1 oz. Chambord
½ oz. Strawberry Leroux
7 oz. Martini Glass
Sprite
Strawberry Jelly
Shaker
Ice

Put liquor, Sprite and ice in the shaker. Stir. Rim strawberry jelly around edge of the martini glass. Strain shaker into martini glass & serve.

Let passion peck you on the lips with the 38th link in the chain of love that I bring to you. Try the kiss that will last a lifetime with your loved one! My special someone and I drank ours together, you should too.

Others who have finished this drink have signed either this paper or the previous page and dated it, in remembrance of family, good friends, great beverages and countless memories to which this drink was made to salute. So when you enjoy a Strawberry Kiss do so by thinking of all the good times we share together. Sincerely Erik G. Ossimina (E.G.O.), a.k.a. Suave

<u>Snake Eye's</u>

Snake Eye's

1 oz. Absolute Vodka
1 oz. Kahlua
Bailey's Irish Cream
2 - 1½ oz. Shot Glasses
Medicine Dropper

Pour ½ oz. of Absolute into each shot glass followed by ½ oz. of Kahlua on top. Take medicine dropper and fill with Bailey's Irish Cream. Unload medicine dropper into top of shot making the appearance of an eye. Then drop a little Kahlua into the Bailey's Irish Cream for the pupil using the medicine dropper.

Glance into the snake's eyes but beware of his fangs. For this snake bites! Snake Eye's is a wonderful shot to have alone or with a friend. Quite possibly you'll drink it with a complete stranger and gain a new friend. You only have to have one shot to sign but I won't stop you from having additional. Snake Eye's is my 39th drink. So stare the snake in his eyes and slam this one down!

Others who have finished this drink have signed either this paper or the previous page and dated it, in remembrance of family, good friends, great beverages and countless memories to which this drink was made to salute. So when you enjoy a Snake Eye's do so by thinking of all the good times we share together. Sincerely Erik G. Ossimina (E.G.O.), a.k.a. Suave

Golden Apple

Golden Apple

½ oz. Goldschlager
½ oz. Apple Barrel Schnapps
Apple Juice
1½ Shot Glass
Apple Slice

Pour Goldschlager into shot glass followed by the Apple Barrel Schnapps. Add a splash of apple juice. Garnish with a small apple slice. (Dunk apple slice into drink, eat the slice & slam down the shot.)

My wife and I drank the 40th drink together at my bar while discussing life and playing Yahtzee. The Golden Apple feels like you just plucked an apple right off the tree and dunked it in a bowl of melted Red Hots. Just like with the fabled story of Adam and Eve, my wife tempted me to partake in this sinful drink and so I did. Now I tempt you to partake in all the joys life has to offer you and drink the Golden Apple. So I say do anything and everything that makes you smile! For you are the Gods of your own world. May no one deny you of your dreams and all the pleasures that this world has to offer you.

Others who have finished this drink have signed either this paper or the previous page and dated it, in remembrance of family, good friends, great beverages and countless memories to which this drink was made to salute. So when you enjoy a Golden Apple do so by thinking of all the good times we share together. Sincerely Erik G. Ossimina (E.G.O.), a.k.a. Suave

The Signature Series

Others who have finished all 10 drinks on this page have signed either this paper or the next page and dated it, in remembrance of family, good friends, great beverages and countless memories to which these drinks were made to salute. So when you enjoy all of these tasty beverages do so by thinking of all the good times we share. Sincerely Erik G. Ossimina (E.G.O.), a.k.a. Suave

The Signature Series

Golden Peach

Golden Peach

½ oz. Goldschlager
½ oz. Peachtree Schnapps
½ oz. Absolute Vodka
Small Peach Slice
1½ oz. Shot Glass

Pour Absolute then the Goldschlager into shot glass followed by the Peachtree Schnapps. Garnish with small peach slice on edge of glass. (Dunk the peach slice into the drink, eat the slice & slam down the shot.)

The Golden Peach is the 41ˢᵗ drink and is the long lost brother of the Golden Apple. They are actually twins with the Golden Apple being just 9 seconds older. Just like my wife and her brother and for that matter my own twins as well, great things don't just come in small packages but two at a time. So if you enjoyed the Golden Apple I'm sure the Golden Peach is for you!

Others who have finished this drink have signed either this paper or the previous page and dated it, in remembrance of family, good friends, great beverages and countless memories to which this drink was made to salute. So when you enjoy a Golden Peach do so by thinking of all the good times we share together. Sincerely Erik G. Ossimina (E.G.O.), a.k.a. Suave

The Purple Rhino

The Purple Rhino

2 oz. Grape Pucker
2 oz. Skyy Infusions Grape Vodka
Kool Aid (Grape Flavor)
16 oz. Pint Glass
Straw
Ice

Fill pint glass ½ way with ice then pour liquor and fill with grape flavored Kool Aid. Stir with straw and serve.

The Purple Rhino Charges into the list at number 42. For such a large animal he can sneak right up on you, be warned. Just strap a saddle on his back and hold on for a tasty ride. He may start out slow but once he gets going hold onto your hat buckaroo.

Others who have finished this drink have signed either this paper or the previous page and dated it, in remembrance of family, good friends, great beverages and countless memories to which this drink was made to salute. So when you enjoy a Purple Rhino do so by thinking of all the good times we share together. Sincerely Erik G. Ossimina (E.G.O.), a.k.a. Suave

Orange Dream

Orange Dream

2 Scoops Orange Sherbet
1 Bottle Stewarts Orange and Cream
2 oz. Everclear
Whipped Cream
Orange Wheel
Cherry
Straw
24 oz. Hurricane Glass
Orange Sugar Crystals
Blender
1-Cup Crushed Ice
Ice Crusher

Blend sherbet, Everclear, Stewarts Orange and Cream and crushed ice together in a blender. (Keep top of blender loose and allow gas to escape when blending). Pour into the hurricane glass & top with whipped cream. Sprinkle orange sugar crystals on top of whipped cream. Garnish the drink with a cherry and orange wheel. Serve with a straw.

A vision of the number 43 should dance thru your head as you sip this relaxing potion down, because that is where this drinks fits into my famous Signature Series. A delightful and tasty beverage to say the least, why not sit down at the bar and swig it down today!

Others who have finished this drink have signed either this paper or the previous page and dated it, in remembrance of family, good friends, great beverages and countless memories to which this drink was made to salute. So when you enjoy an Orange Dream do so by thinking of all the good times we share together. Sincerely Erik G. Ossimina (E.G.O.), a.k.a. Suave

Butterscotch Bliss

Butterscotch Bliss

2 oz. Butterscotch Schnapps
1 oz. Absolute Vodka
Vanilla Ice Cream
1 Cup Milk
Butterscotch Syrup
12 oz. Rocks Glass
Whipped Cream
Blender
2 Bar Straws
Ice

Blend Schnapps & Vodka with the ice cream and milk in a blender. Next coat the inside of the glass using the syrup. Fill glass halfway with ice and pour blender into the rocks glass. Top with whipped cream. Pour syrup over whipped cream and add straws.

A tasty treat anytime! Just whip out your blender and treat yourself to a wonderful time. Or perhaps you need a pick me up, well look no further friend. I have the goods for you. In the form of a liquid beverage, I bring to you a ray of sunshine on a cloudy morning. My friends, happiness awaits you after every sip. By the way you know that milk is great for your bones, so why not do something that is good for the body, mind and spirit. It might even please your mom; she's always telling you to drink your milk. Now you can tell her your enjoying 2 to 3 glasses of milk a day we'll just forget to tell her what else is accompanying the milk. Butterscotch Bliss is the 44th drink and a yummy one at that!

Others who have finished this drink have signed either this paper or the previous page and dated it, in remembrance of family, good friends, great beverages and countless memories to which this drink was made to salute. So when you enjoy Butterscotch Bliss do so by thinking of all the good times we share together. Sincerely Erik G. Ossimina (E.G.O.), a.k.a. Suave

A Shot In The Dark

A Shot In The Dark

1 oz. Johnnie Walker Black Label
½ oz. Kahlua
1 ½ oz. Shot Glass

In a shot glass pour Johnny Walker and top with Kahlua.

You might want to lower the lights before slamming this one down. A strange sensation will over come you as it slides down your throat. A pleasant mixture of spine tingling madness with a side of hot flashes will no doubt put a smile on your face. Number 45, A Shot in the Dark, is just one step away from you!

Others who have finished this drink have signed either this paper or the previous page and dated it, in remembrance of family, good friends, great beverages and countless memories to which this drink was made to salute. So when you enjoy A Shot In The Dark do so by thinking of all the good times we share together. Sincerely Erik G. Ossimina (E.G.O.), a.k.a. Suave

Blushing Bride

Blushing Bride

1 oz. Absolute Vodka
2 oz. Godiva "white chocolate Liqueur"
1 oz. Amaretto
Grenadine
Milk
Ice
12 oz. White Wine Glass
1½ oz. Shot glass
Straw

Fill wine glass halfway with ice and add the Absolute and Godiva, followed by filling the rest of the glass an inch away from the top with milk. Put amaretto in shot glass with a splash of Grenadine. Serve shot glass as a sidecar to the wine glass. Have patron dump the shot into the wine glass and stir to make the bride blush.

Let my 46th drink bring you back to that special day or perhaps to the possibility of having your own day in the sun. Whether in the past, present or future the Blushing Bride will always bring a little joy to the drinker. Do you remember back to the days when you still might blush or when your wife used to? Enjoying this one might make you blush as well.

Others who have finished this drink have signed either this paper or the previous page and dated it, in remembrance of family, good friends, great beverages and countless memories to which this drink was made to salute. So when you enjoy Blushing Bride do so by thinking of all the good times we share together. Sincerely Erik G. Ossimina (E.G.O.), a.k.a. Suave

Honey Bee

Honey Bee

1 oz. Absolute Vodka
Honey
1½ Shot Glass

Pour vodka into shot glass and fill with honey.

Drink up like you're a bear raiding the hive. Have shots till you fall down with this one! This is the 47ᵗʰ drink and is sure to delight all who partake in the joys of being stung. I know I do. Speaking of getting stung, I remember back when I was a young lad around the tender age of 5 or so. I saw a ball stuck in a tree and decided to free it with a stick that was lying on the ground. What a surprise to find out that in fact the ball was not a ball at all but a bee hive full of angry bees. The bees where everywhere! They were stuck in my hair and stinging me at every turn. Luckily my Mom was there to save me. Thanks Mom. So let's raise our glasses and give a toast to Mom's everywhere for without them where would we bee.

Others who have finished this drink have signed either this paper or the previous page and dated it, in remembrance of family, good friends, great beverages and countless memories to which this drink was made to salute. So when you enjoy a Honey Bee do so by thinking of all the good times we share together. Sincerely Erik G. Ossimina (E.G.O.), a.k.a. Suave

Captain Jack

Captain Jack

1 ½ oz. Captain Morgan
1 ½ oz. Jack Daniels
Pepsi
16 oz. Pint Glass
Ice
Lime
Straw

Pour the alcohol into the pint glass, followed by some ice. Then fill with Pepsi. Garnish with lime and straw.

Captain Jack docks his boat at number 48. A tasty combination of Captain Morgan and Jack Daniels brings the Captain to life. So set sail with Captain Jack at the helm. Your evening will be chock-full of great times in a wonderful atmosphere where friends are made and remembered. Let those who oppose us walk the plank! Arg!!!

Others who have finished this drink have signed either this paper or the previous page and dated it, in remembrance of family, good friends, great beverages and countless memories to which this drink was made to salute. So when you enjoy Captain Jack do so by thinking of all the good times we share together. Sincerely Erik G. Ossimina (E.G.O.), a.k.a. Suave

The Widow Maker

The Widow Maker

Bartles and James Strawberry Wine Cooler
1 oz. Absolute Vodka
1 oz. Southern Comfort
1 oz. Gordon's Gin
Sprite
16 oz. Pint Glass
Ice

Pour the Absolute, Southern Comfort and Gordon's into the pint glass. Next add a hand full of ice. Fill remaining space with an equal mixture of Bartles and James wine cooler and sprite.

The Widow Maker is no joke! So enjoy with caution especially if your wife or girlfriend have made it for you. This is # 49th drink & only one more drink to go and we'll be halfway there, that's if you can get past this one.

Others who have finished this drink have signed either this paper or the previous page and dated it, in remembrance of family, good friends, great beverages and countless memories to which this drink was made to salute. So when you enjoy The Widow Maker do so by thinking of all the good times we share together. Sincerely Erik G. Ossimina (E.G.O.), a.k.a. Suave

The Agitator

The Agitator

1 oz. Absolute Vodka
½ oz. Chartreuse
1 ½ oz. Shot Glass

Pour Absolute into the shot glass and then top with Chartreuse. Let chill in freezer. Serve shot cold.

My dad introduced me to Chartreuse and now I present it to you in my own little special way. What a drink to top off the first 50 drinks. Only 50 more to go and I bet you wonder what I will have in store for you. Don't worry about that now; first you have the agitator to deal with. Prepare your stomach for an agitation like you have not experienced before. I found that a nice straight shot of Bailey's Irish Cream is quite nice afterwards. However I think you should see for yourself.

Others who have finished this drink have signed either this paper or the previous page and dated it, in remembrance of family, good friends, great beverages and countless memories to which this drink was made to salute. So when you enjoy The Agitator do so by thinking of all the good times we share together. Sincerely Erik G. Ossimina (E.G.O.), a.k.a. Suave

The Signature Series

Others who have finished all 10 drinks on this page have signed either this paper or the next page and dated it, in remembrance of family, good friends, great beverages and countless memories to which these drinks were made to salute. So when you enjoy all of these tasty beverages do so by thinking of all the good times we share. Sincerely Erik G. Ossimina (E.G.O.), a.k.a. Suave

The Signature Series

124

The Body Cleanser

The Body Cleanser

½ oz. Absolute Vodka
½ oz. Bacardi Light Rum
½ oz. Strawberry Leroux
1½ oz. Shot Glass

Fill shot glass with Absolute and Bacardi using the Strawberry Leroux to top off the shot.

A warm sensation will fill your body with this shot so brace yourself. This shot will clean you from the inside out, especially after the 8th or 9th shot. This is the 51st drink and from now on I will just put the number of the drink in the beginning of the paragraph.

Others who have finished this drink have signed either this paper or the previous page and dated it, in remembrance of family, good friends, great beverages and countless memories to which this drink was made to salute. So when you enjoy The Body Cleanser do so by thinking of all the good times we share together. Sincerely Erik G. Ossimina (E.G.O.), a.k.a. Suave

Eliminator

Eliminator

1 oz. Johnnie Walker
1 oz. Jack Daniels
1 oz. Absolute Vodka
1 oz. Everclear
Pepsi
16 oz. Pint Glass
Ice
Lime Wedge
Cherry
Straw
Cocktail Sword

Fill pint glass ½ way with ice. Add liquor and fill with Pepsi. Stir. For the garnish stab cherry and lime with cocktail sword and hang on edge of the glass.

#52 All I can say is that you will be eliminated after finishing this one! Not intended for the inexperienced drinker! This drink is for the experienced connoisseur. So if you want hair on your chest and maybe even on your tongue I invite you to get eliminated! Pepsi is the signature cola of The Signature Series & if Pepsi would like to thank me for that feel free to contact me. Here's a new slogan for ya:

Pepsi the choice of every Generation!

Others who have finished this drink have signed either this paper or the previous page and dated it, in remembrance of family, good friends, great beverages and countless memories to which this drink was made to salute. So when you enjoy an Eliminator do so by thinking of all the good times we share together. Sincerely Erik G. Ossimina (E.G.O.), a.k.a. Suave

Strawberry Lemonade

Strawberry Lemonade

1 oz. Strawberry Leroux
2 oz. Smirnoff Strawberry Twist
Country Time Lemonade
16 oz. Pint Glass
Ice
Straw
Strawberry
Lemon Wedge

Fill pint glass ½ way with ice. Add liquor and fill with lemonade. Stir with straw and garnish with strawberry and lemon wedge.

#53 A nice way to start or finish an evening, Strawberry lemonade will put you in the mood to sit back and relax. Not too strong, just the right bite to keep you interested. A great drink to take down to the pool to enjoy while you put your feet up and catch some rays.

Others who have finished this drink have signed either this paper or the previous page and dated it, in remembrance of family, good friends, great beverages and countless memories to which this drink was made to salute. So when you enjoy a Strawberry Lemonade do so by thinking of all the good times we share together. Sincerely Erik G. Ossimina (E.G.O.), a.k.a. Suave

Trash Can

Trash Can

1 oz. Absolute Vodka
1 oz. Jack Daniels
1 oz. Captain Morgan
1 oz. Southern Comfort
1 oz. Bacardi
1 oz. Johnnie Walker
1 oz. Seagram's VO
23 oz. Pilsner
Pepsi
Ice
Straw
Assorted Fruits

Throw your liquor, ice and Pepsi into a tallboy. Stir with a straw and top with assorted fruits or other leftovers.

#54 Take your time with this one or you might just end up in a trash can. Head my advice, take care when sipping this one down. This is a potent drink and should be handled as so. It is like enjoying three drinks at once. Take it slow and steady, as you should do with all beverages that contain multiple amounts of liquor. Or slam it down and we'll all have plenty of photos and stories for the years to come.

Others who have finished this drink have signed either this paper or the previous page and dated it, in remembrance of family, good friends, great beverages and countless memories to which this drink was made to salute. So when you enjoy a Trash Can do so by thinking of all the good times we share together. Sincerely Erik G. Ossimina (E.G.O.), a.k.a. Suave

A Sinfully Sweet Sensation

A Sinfully Sweet Sensation

1 oz. Godiva
½ oz. Bailey's Irish Cream
1 ½ oz. Shot Glass
Whipped Cream
Chocolate Shavings
Spoon

Pour 1 oz. of Godiva into a shot glass. Then using a spoon float the Bailey's Irish Cream. Top with a small blast of whipped cream followed with a sprinkle of chocolate shavings.

#55 Will certainly give you a little pick me up. A great way to zest up any party, just make a tray full and watch them disappear. Also known as Triple S or ASSS for short. A great host will always be at the ready with this in their repertoire of drinks. For it is effortless to make, at the same time looks and tastes great. A sure winner to put your next party over the top!

Others who have finished this drink have signed either this paper or the previous page and dated it, in remembrance of family, good friends, great beverages and countless memories to which this drink was made to salute. So when you enjoy A Sinfully Sweet Sensation do so by thinking of all the good times we share together. Sincerely Erik G. Ossimina (E.G.O.), a.k.a. Suave

Ecstasy

Ecstasy

1 oz. Brown Crème de Cacao
1 oz. Godiva
1 oz. Bailey's Irish Cream
1 oz. Kahlua
Milk
12 oz. Rocks Glass
Shaker
Straw
Ice

Pour liquor into the rocks glass, add ice then fill with milk. Empty into shaker and shake it up. Dispense back into rocks glass and add two bar straws.

#56 The name says it all. For your lips will tremble in shear delight after each and every sip. This in my opinion is the perfect drink to get anyone in the mood for a night of debauchery or just sitting around with loved ones singing church hymns. Whatever floats your boat! Just be sure to have enough for everyone. This one is addicting!

Others who have finished this drink have signed either this paper or the previous page and dated it, in remembrance of family, good friends, great beverages and countless memories to which this drink was made to salute. So when you enjoy Ecstasy do so by thinking of all the good times we share together. Sincerely Erik G. Ossimina (E.G.O.), a.k.a. Suave

Sunrise Sunset

Sunrise Sunset

1 oz. Absolute
1 oz. Grand Marnier
Orange Juice
Champagne
12 oz. White Wine Glass
Ice

Pour liquor into wine glass. Add ice and fill glass with 1 part Champagne and 2 parts orange juice.

#57 A tasty treat to celebrate the rise and fall of the sun. This is the mimosa of a new age. Enjoy it during the sunrise and wake up at sunset. Breakfast will never be the same! Start your mornings off right with a new classic and give a toast to the sun, the real reason for the season!

Others who have finished this drink have signed either this paper or the previous page and dated it, in remembrance of family, good friends, great beverages and countless memories to which this drink was made to salute. So when you enjoy Sunrise Sunset do so by thinking of all the good times we share together. Sincerely Erik G. Ossimina (E.G.O.), a.k.a. Suave

Crazy Hawaiian

Crazy Hawaiian

1 ½ oz. Tangueray
1 ½ oz. Blue Curacao
1 oz Absolute Vodka
Pineapple Juice
Orange Juice
Grenadine
16 oz. Pint Glass
1½ oz. Shot Glass
Ice
Pineapple Chunk
Tbs. Sugar
Straw

Pour Tangueray and Blue Curacao into your pint glass. Follow with ice, sugar, orange and pineapple juices. Stir. Leaving room to add a shot to the drink. Put a small pineapple chunk on side of pint glass. Pour vodka and Grenadine into a shot glass. Serve the shot glass with the drink as a sidecar. Let patron pour shot into drink.

#58 The Crazy Hawaiian is great at a luau or any party. Watch as the drink turns color before your eyes as you add the sidecar to your drink. Just grab some leis and get ready to party with the Crazy Hawaiian!

Others who have finished this drink have signed either this paper or the previous page and dated it, in remembrance of family, good friends, great beverages and countless memories to which this drink was made to salute. So when you enjoy a Crazy Hawaiian do so by thinking of all the good times we share together. Sincerely Erik G. Ossimina (E.G.O.), a.k.a. Suave

Jersey Juice

Jersey Juice

1 oz. Apple Schnapps
1 oz. Peach Schnapps
1 oz. Watermelon Schnapps
1 oz. Strawberry Leroux
Cranberry Juice
Orange Juice
Umbrella
Orange slice
Cherry
Straw
Ice
16 oz. Pint Glass
Shaker

Pour all of the Schnapps into a shaker with ice. Next add 2 parts cranberry juice and 1 part orange juice to fill shaker. Shake. Empty shaker into pint glass and garnish with cherry, orange slice and umbrella. Serve with a straw.

#59 Jersey Juice is a refreshing beverage for all to enjoy. Not to strong, just enough kick to get you going. Let the juices flow into your mouth with each sip. Weather you're sunning yourself at L.B.I. or hanging in Ho Ho Kus or kicking it in Jackson. You will rejoice after enjoying this one.

Others who have finished this drink have signed either this paper or the previous page and dated it, in remembrance of family, good friends, great beverages and countless memories to which this drink was made to salute. So when you enjoy Jersey Juice do so by thinking of all the good times we share together. Sincerely Erik G. Ossimina (E.G.O.), a.k.a. Suave

33 Cups Of Madness

33 Cups Of Madness

1 Cup Crystal Head Vodka
¼ Cup Jack Daniels
1 - 16 oz. Amp Energy Lightning
3 Cups A.M. Orange-Strawberry Gatorade
Country Time Lemonade
33 Plastic Cups
1 Beer Pitcher
1 Plastic Pitcher
Big Spoon

Make lemonade in the plastic pitcher and chill ahead of time. In the beer pitcher pour alcohol, Amp energy drink and Gatorade, filling with lemonade. Stir. Empty the pitcher equally into the 33 plastic cups. Who ever drinks the most cups wins. In the event of a tie whoever finished first wins.

#60 is a drinking game for 4 or more people to play. The more people the faster the game. Arrange cups close together on a table where everyone playing has enough room to reach all the cups. Collect the cups as you drink them. When the last cup is finished whoever has the most cups wins. Now you can try the slow & steady method or just slam em down. I went for the slam em down, get the lead then just keep pace method. But somehow I was outdone by the slow and steady method and lost by one cup! I thought I was easily ahead and didn't realize until it was too late that I was over taken. It reminds me of the old story of the tortoise and hare. So keep an eye on your opponents, especially if they have a shell on their back. Dirty Tortoise! Be the first one to cross the finish line with the most cups in your hand!

Others who have finished this drink have signed either this paper or the previous page and dated it, in remembrance of family, good friends, great beverages and countless memories to which this drink was made to salute. So when you enjoy 33 Cups Of Madness do so by thinking of all the good times we share together. Sincerely Erik G. Ossimina (E.G.O.), a.k.a. Suave

The Signature Series

Others who have finished all 10 drinks on this page have signed either this paper or the next page and dated it, in remembrance of family, good friends, great beverages and countless memories to which these drinks were made to salute. So when you enjoy all of these tasty beverages do so by thinking of all the good times we share. Sincerely Erik G. Ossimina (E.G.O.), a.k.a. Suave

The Signature Series

Jumping Java

Jumping Java

Folgers Classic Roast
1 oz. White Cream De Cocoa
½ oz. Patron XO Café
Coffee Cup
Milk
Spoon
Coffee Maker

Brew Folgers Classic Roast in a coffee maker. Pour liquor into a coffee cup followed with the freshly brewed coffee. Add milk to taste and stir.

#61 Is coffee with a kick! My wife's hands trembled just after having two sips causing her to spill coffee on her bosoms. So be careful with this hot beverage, I wouldn't want any more accidents to occur! Jumping Java was made to be a great drink to end an evening with or possibly you might prefer to start your morning off instead. Whichever time you choose to enjoy Jumping Java, I'm sure it will put you in the right frame of mind.

Others who have finished this drink have signed either this paper or the previous page and dated it, in remembrance of family, good friends, great beverages and countless memories to which this drink was made to salute. So when you enjoy a Jumping Java do so by thinking of all the good times we share together. Sincerely Erik G. Ossimina (E.G.O.), a.k.a. Suave

Strawberry Banana Banshee

Strawberry Banana Banshee

2 oz. Strawberry Leroux
2 oz. 99 Bananas
2 oz. Absolute Vodka
Banana
Strawberries
6 – 12 oz. Rocks Glasses
Sip Straws
Blender
2 Cups Milk
Ice

Put 2 cups of milk and liquor into the blender. Then add a handful of strawberries and half of a banana. With the other half of banana cut 6 banana wheels for garnish, if any banana remains toss it into the blender. Blend until mixture is uniformly smooth. Fill the rocks glasses with ice then pour in your blended mixture. For the garnish put a banana wheel and a strawberry slice on the side of the glass. Serve with two sip straws. (Makes 6 drinks)

 # 62 Will send a shiver down your spine. It has also been said to heal the throat after a mind blowing sonic scream. (The Banshees greatest known power) This secret drink is now available for all to enjoy!

Others who have finished this drink have signed either this paper or the previous page and dated it, in remembrance of family, good friends, great beverages and countless memories to which this drink was made to salute. So when you enjoy a Strawberry Banana Banshee do so by thinking of all the good times we share together. Sincerely Erik G. Ossimina (E.G.O.), a.k.a. Suave

Fruit Basket

Fruit Basket

Splash Of Absolute Vodka
Splash Of Strawberry Leroux
Splash Of Dr. Mcgillicuddy's Cherry Schnapps
Cherry
Strawberry
Orange Wheel
1½ oz. Shot Glass
Knife
Cherry juice

Cut strawberry, orange wheel and cherry into small pieces. Put pieces into shot glass. Then add a splash of each of the liquors and finish shot with a splash of cherry juice.

#63 A tasty treat! The Fruit Basket takes having a shot to a new level. In the mood to do multiple shots, but don't want to deal with the harshness of most. Well this is your shot. The fruity flavors will make any shot aficionado smile☺

Others who have finished this drink have signed either this paper or the previous page and dated it, in remembrance of family, good friends, great beverages and countless memories to which this drink was made to salute. So when you enjoy a Fruit Basket do so by thinking of all the good times we share together. Sincerely Erik G. Ossimina (E.G.O.), a.k.a. Suave

The Bloody Bitch

The Bloody Bitch

1/2 oz. Yago Sant Gria
1/2 oz. Sprite
1/2oz. Absolute Vodka
Grenadine
Fancy Stemmed 1½ oz. Shot Glass
Shaker
Ice

Put vodka, Sprite and Yago Sant Gria into the shaker filled with ice. While shaker is chilling, coat rim of the shot glass with Grenadine. Once shaker is chilled strain into the fancy stemmed shot glass.

#64 Another great shot with an awesome taste to bring your spirits to a new level. The Bloody Bitch can also be enjoyed on the rocks if you like. Just break out the rocks glasses put 1½ oz. vodka with 5 oz's of Yago Sant Gria and fill with Sprite. But to sign this paper, you must have the shot the way the drink was originally intended. Watch out how many you have because the Bloody Bitch has a way of sneaking up on you. If your not careful you might end up bloody yourself!

Others who have finished this drink have signed either this paper or the previous page and dated it, in remembrance of family, good friends, great beverages and countless memories to which this drink was made to salute. So when you enjoy The Bloody Bitch do so by thinking of all the good times we share together. Sincerely Erik G. Ossimina (E.G.O.), a.k.a. Suave

Butterscotch Daiquiri

Butterscotch Daiquiri

3½ oz. Bacardi
2½ oz. Butterscotch Schnapps
Butterscotch Syrup
Shaker
7 oz. Martini Glass
Ice

Squirt butterscotch syrup into shaker. Add ice and liquor to shaker. Shake. Drizzle the butterscotch syrup around the inside of the martini glass. Strain shaker into the glass and serve.

 # 65 Quick, easy and tasty! What more could you want in a drink? Be sure to stock up on the butterscotch syrup and schnapps. In my experience they go fast. This is my favorite non-frozen daiquiri to date!

Others who have finished this drink have signed either this paper or the previous page and dated it, in remembrance of family, good friends, great beverages and countless memories to which this drink was made to salute. So when you enjoy a Butterscotch Daiquiri do so by thinking of all the good times we share together. Sincerely Erik G. Ossimina (E.G.O.), a.k.a. Suave

Orange Mojito

Orange Mojito

1 oz. Bacardi 151
1 oz. Grand Marnier
Club Soda
Orange Juice
1 Tbs. Sugar
Crushed Ice
Orange wedge
Orange Slice
Lime wedge
Mint Sprig
Muddler
Spoon
Straw
14 oz. Collins Glass
Shaker

Muddle in your shaker an orange and lime wedges, some mint leafs and 1 tablespoon of sugar. Add ice and liquor. Shake. Empty shaker into Collins glass and add a splash of club soda then fill with orange juice. Serve with a straw. Use orange slice, lime wedge and mint sprig as your garnish.

 # 66 is a great drink to serve at any dinner party. The Orange Mojito will not disappoint.

Others who have finished this drink have signed either this paper or the previous page and dated it, in remembrance of family, good friends, great beverages and countless memories to which this drink was made to salute. So when you enjoy an Orange Mojito do so by thinking of all the good times we share together. Sincerely Erik G. Ossimina (E.G.O.), a.k.a. Suave

Saint's or Sinner's Punch

Saint's or Sinner's Punch

Saint's or Sinner's Punch

Saints:

6 oz. Pineapple Juice
2 Cups Orange Juice
2 Cups Cranberry Juice
½ Cup Christian Brothers Brandy VS
¼ Tablespoons of Sugar
½ Cup Strawberry Leroux
12 oz. Sprite
Beer Pitcher
12 oz. Rocks Glass
Orange
Strawberries
Raspberries
Lemon
Lime
Ice

Sinners Add:

½ oz. Bacardi 151
½ oz. Bacardi Gold
½ oz. Absolute Citron
16 oz. Beer Mug
Straw
Ice

For the <u>Saint's Punch</u>: No ice in the pitcher. Pour the brandy, Strawberry Leroux and sugar into the pitcher followed with pineapple juice, orange juice, cranberry juice and Sprite. Stir. Cut a lemon, lime and orange into a wheel and then into fours. Also slice strawberries and raspberries into chunks and put into pitcher. Serve in rocks glasses full of ice. Add 2 small bar straws. Keep pitcher refrigerated when not serving.

For the <u>Sinners Punch</u>: Fill beer mug with ice, then add Bacardi 151, Bacardi Gold and Absolute Citron. Finally fill your mug from the pitcher.

#'S 67 & 68 have arrived. Looking for a punch that is a real knockout. Well here are two variations one for Saints and one for Sinners. Saints sign in blue and Sinners in red! Who dares to drink them both? This is great to make the night before any party or gathering. Your guests will be thrilled with having the choice between the two. So drink up and sign below space is limited!

Others who have finished this drink have signed either this paper or the previous page and dated it, in remembrance of family, good friends, great beverages and countless memories to which this drink was made to salute. So when you enjoy Saint's or Sinner's Punch do so by thinking of all the good times we share together. Sincerely Erik G. Ossimina (E.G.O.), a.k.a. Suave

Tidal Wave

Tidal Wave

2 oz. Blue Curacao
2 oz. Cabo Wabo Tequila
Ice Crusher
3 Cups Crushed Ice
¼ Cup Coco Lopez
1-Cup Milk
Blender
24 oz. Hurricane Glass
Whipped Cream
Cherry
Straw

In a blender pour liquor followed by milk, ice and Coco Lopez. Blend until mixture is uniformly even. Pour contents of blender into glass. Add a straw, whipped cream and a cherry.

 # 69 Will this wave be hard to paddle through? There is only one way to find out, so man up and get out there. Ride the wave of intoxication! Just don't let it crash down upon you. Have Fun!

Others who have finished this drink have signed either this paper or the previous page and dated it, in remembrance of family, good friends, great beverages and countless memories to which this drink was made to salute. So when you enjoy a Tidal Wave do so by thinking of all the good times we share together. Sincerely Erik G. Ossimina (E.G.O.), a.k.a. Suave

The Terrible Tiki

The Terrible Tiki

1 oz. Bacardi 151
1 oz. Bacardi Gold
½ oz. Triple Sec
½ oz. Sloe Gin
10 oz. Tiki Mug or Larger

Crushed Ice
Umbrella
Shaker

2½ oz. Orange Juice
2½ oz. Pineapple Juice
Orange Wheel
Ice Crusher
Cherry

Straw
Ice

Put all liquor and juices into shaker. Shake thoroughly. Fill Tiki most of the way with crushed ice. Then pour contents of the shaker into your Tiki. Add straw, orange wheel, cherry and umbrella for garnish and serve.

#70 The Terrible Tiki doesn't get its name from its taste. It is said that the Powerful Tiki will forever torment those who dare drink and don't finish! This drink is the perfect reason to go out and find a couple of great Tiki mugs for your bar or home. In my version of the classic Polynesian treat you will never have to sacrifice great taste, just uniformity. So bring the sprit of the Tiki into your home!

Others who have finished this drink have signed either this paper or the previous page and dated it, in remembrance of family, good friends, great beverages and countless memories to which this drink was made to salute. So when you enjoy The Terrible Tiki do so by thinking of all the good times we share together. Sincerely Erik G. Ossimina (E.G.O.), a.k.a. Suave

The Signature Series

Others who have finished all 10 drinks on this page have signed either this paper or the next page and dated it, in remembrance of family, good friends, great beverages and countless memories to which these drinks were made to salute. So when you enjoy all of these tasty beverages do so by thinking of all the good times we share. Sincerely Erik G. Ossimina (E.G.O.), a.k.a. Suave

The Signature Series

Cookies & Cream

Cookies & Cream

2 oz. Godiva "white Chocolate liquor"
3½ oz. Heavy Cream
1 oz. Crushed Oreo
7 oz. Martini Glass
Whipped Cream
Muddler
Shaker
Ice

Crush Oreos in the shaker using a Muddler until you have 1 oz. crushed Oreo. Put the crushed Oreos into the martini glass leaving ½ a teaspoon or so for the garnish. Next put ice into the shaker and add the Godiva and heavy cream. Shake. Let chill, then pour the shaker into the martini glass. Spray whipped cream on one side of the glass and sprinkle the remaining crushed Oreo on top of whipped cream.

#71 A tasty treat that can be enjoyed any time of the day, but may I suggest serving as an after dinner drink. Your guests will be enchanted and I'm sure some great conversation will follow.

Others who have finished this drink have signed either this paper or the previous page and dated it, in remembrance of family, good friends, great beverages and countless memories to which this drink was made to salute. So when you enjoy Cookies & Cream do so by thinking of all the good times we share together. Sincerely Erik G. Ossimina (E.G.O.), a.k.a. Suave

TNT

1 oz. Tangueray
1 oz. Triple Sec
½ oz. Everclear
Orange Juice
12 oz. Rocks Glass
2 Sip Straws
Lemon Wheel
2 Raspberries
Cocktail Sword
Ice

Fill rocks glass with ice. Pour Everclear, Tangueray and Triple Sec into the rocks glass. Fill with orange juice. Cut lemon wheel into three pieces. Stab sword into lemon then raspberry then lemon then raspberry and finally the lemon and float on top of the drink. Serve with 2 sip straws.

 # 72 is ready to explode at any moment with great taste. This isn't your Father's old version of TNT. The new and improved TNT will totally live up to its name! While my wife and I were reviewing the book for final review, "Concrete shoes, cyanide, TNT done dirt-cheap" blasted from my radio at the same time we got to this drink. AC/ DC definitely will knock your socks off and are the perfect band to listen to while you enjoy this one.

Others who have finished this drink have signed either this paper or the previous page and dated it, in remembrance of family, good friends, great beverages and countless memories to which this drink was made to salute. So when you enjoy TNT do so by thinking of all the good times we share together. Sincerely Erik G. Ossimina (E.G.O.), a.k.a. Suave

The Golden Goose

The Golden Goose

½ oz. Goldschlager
1 oz. Grey Goose Vodka
Lemon Juice
1½ Shot Glass

Pour vodka into shot glass. Follow with Goldschlager and top off with a splash of lemon juice.

#73 Is a great shot to get things going. Your palate will be excited for anything else the night might have in store after shooting down a couple Golden Geese. This drink will be your golden egg not a goose egg I promise you! I know you don't care how you want it now!

Others who have finished this drink have signed either this paper or the previous page and dated it, in remembrance of family, good friends, great beverages and countless memories to which this drink was made to salute. So when you enjoy a Golden Goose do so by thinking of all the good times we share together. Sincerely Erik G. Ossimina (E.G.O.), a.k.a. Suave

172

East Of Eden

East Of Eden

4 oz. Grape Pucker
2 oz. Jose Cuervo Tequila
2 Cups Glacier Freeze Gatorade
Ice Crusher
Ice
Blender
Straw
24 oz. Hurricane Glass

Crush ice and mix all ingredients in blender. Blend for a minute, then pour into hurricane glass. Serve with a straw.

#74 This is as close to Eden as most of you will ever get! Well at least you're not south of Eden I guess. East of Eden will delight all those who sip this one down. So get in line and try one today.

Others who have finished this drink have signed either this paper or the previous page and dated it, in remembrance of family, good friends, great beverages and countless memories to which this drink was made to salute. So when you enjoy East Of Eden do so by thinking of all the good times we share together. Sincerely Erik G. Ossimina (E.G.O.), a.k.a. Suave

Creamy Manhattan

Creamy Manhattan

2 oz. Seagram's VO
½ oz. Sweet Vermouth
2 oz. White Crème de Cacao
2 oz. Heavy Cream
7 oz. Martini Glass
Cocoa Powder
Shaker
Ice

Other than cocoa powder put all ingredients into the shaker. Shake it like you mean it, then strain into martini glass. Sprinkle a few dashes of cocoa powder on top of drink as a garnish.

 # 75 If your drinking my drinks in order then your ¾th's of the way there. Way to go! What a tremendous drink to take this spot. I have tried to bring the Manhattan to a new level. I am sure that this new classic will soon be available everywhere!

Others who have finished this drink have signed either this paper or the previous page and dated it, in remembrance of family, good friends, great beverages and countless memories to which this drink was made to salute. So when you enjoy a Creamy Manhattan do so by thinking of all the good times we share together. Sincerely Erik G. Ossimina (E.G.O.), a.k.a. Suave

Electric Storm

Electric Storm

1 oz. Everclear
1 oz. Absolute Citron
1 oz. Blue Curacao
Lemonade
16 oz. Beer Mug
Lemon Wedge
Sprite
Ice
Straw
1½ oz. Shot glass
Shaker

Pour Everclear and Absolute Citron into shaker with ice. Then put lemon wedge into the shot glass followed by the Blue Curacao. Fill shaker with lemonade and shake vigorously. Empty shaker into beer mug and top with a layer of Sprite. Serve beer mug with a straw and the shot on the side. Let the patron put the lemon into his or her drink followed by the rest of the shot.

#76 Shocking and electrifying this drink is so smooth it will take you to places you have never been before. Prepare yourself for a rough night cause a storm is definitely coming! Slow at first, but by the time you're on your 2nd or 3rd one you'll know that the storm is here and it's Electrifying!

Others who have finished this drink have signed either this paper or the previous page and dated it, in remembrance of family, good friends, great beverages and countless memories to which this drink was made to salute. So when you enjoy an Electric Storm do so by thinking of all the good times we share together. Sincerely Erik G. Ossimina (E.G.O.), a.k.a. Suave

Strawberry Cream Delight

Strawberry Cream Delight

4 oz. Bacardi
1 ½ Cup Mr. & Mrs. T "Strawberry Daiquiri Margarita Mix"
½ Cup Heavy Cream
1-Cup Crushed Ice
24 oz. Hurricane Glass
Whipped Cream
Red Sugar Crystals
Blender
Straw

Fill blender with Bacardi, margarita mix, crushed ice and heavy cream. Blend thoroughly. Pour into hurricane glass. Spray whipped cream on top along with the sugar crystals. Add a straw.

 # 77
Strawberry Cream Delight
My drink is out of sight!
I say drink one down tonight.
& everything will be all right.
Unless you take mine, then we will fight.
You will see the light.
So don't get in a fright
Just do what's right.
Enjoy your own Strawberry Cream Delight!
& may everyone have an intoxicating night!

Others who have finished this drink have signed either this paper or the previous page and dated it, in remembrance of family, good friends, great beverages and countless memories to which this drink was made to salute. So when you enjoy a Strawberry Cream Delight do so by thinking of all the good times we share together. Sincerely Erik G. Ossimina (E.G.O.), a.k.a. Suave

Lady Bug

Lady Bug

Mike's Hard Cranberry
Yago Sant Gria
1 oz. Southern Comfort
12 oz. White Wine Glass
Ice
Blue Berries

Fill your wine glass with ice and blueberries (The blue berries will act as the spots on the lady bug). **Next add Southern Comfort and fill with one part Yago Sant Gria and two parts Mike's Hard Cranberry.**

#78 Enjoy the Lady Bug instead of a second-rate wine. When others break out a box of wine, simply tell them to subscribe to a new way of life. Introduce them to something far more superior for them to take pleasure in. They can even eat the berries when they finish the drink. Insist on the best for you and your guests! I always do.

Others who have finished this drink have signed either this paper or the previous page and dated it, in remembrance of family, good friends, great beverages and countless memories to which this drink was made to salute. So when you enjoy a Lady Bug do so by thinking of all the good times we share together. Sincerely Erik G. Ossimina (E.G.O.), a.k.a. Suave

Berry Bonanza

Berry Bonanza

½ oz. Blackberry Brandy
½ oz. Chambord
½ oz. Sloe Gin
½ oz. Strawberry Leroux
½ oz. 99 Berries
1 oz. Absolute Vodka
Raspberry
Blackberries
Strawberry
Cocktail Stick
Sprite
16 oz. Pint Glass
Ice
Straw

Pour liquor into pint glass followed with ice and Sprite. Next using your cocktail stick pierce berries keeping the strawberry on the top. Then place in glass and serve.

 # 79 The name says it all. If you like berries this is the drink for you. I suggest dunking the garnish into the drink then eating it. But that's just me. You do what you will.

Others who have finished this drink have signed either this paper or the previous page and dated it, in remembrance of family, good friends, great beverages and countless memories to which this drink was made to salute. So when you enjoy Berry Bonanza do so by thinking of all the good times we share together. Sincerely Erik G. Ossimina (E.G.O.), a.k.a. Suave

Mixed Melon Chiller

185

Mixed Melon Chiller

3 oz. White Wine
5 oz. Sprite
½ oz. Smirnoff Watermelon Twist
½ oz. Midori
12 oz. White Wine Glass
Ice

Pour Smirnoff and Midori into the wine glass; add ice followed by portions of wine and Sprite.

#80 Another drink that is easy enough to make. Use your favorite white wine. Perfect for poolside chatter or just passing time away in a lawn chair. Feel free to change this drink into a Mixed Melon Spritzer by substituting the Sprite with club soda. I prefer it with Sprite. The Mixed Melon Spritzer is drink #101. It's not on the list, but hidden here. Think of it as an extra little something. Maybe the Mixed Melon Spritzer could be the answer for a trivia question, what is the 101st drink in the Signature Series? If you answered Lucky Lefty's Luscious Licorice Liquor Lift you would be wrong. So when you enjoy the Mixed Melon Spritzer sign this page with a star next to your name, so everyone will know which one you had.

Others who have finished this drink have signed either this paper or the previous page and dated it, in remembrance of family, good friends, great beverages and countless memories to which this drink was made to salute. So when you enjoy a Mixed Melon Chiller do so by thinking of all the good times we share together. Sincerely Erik G. Ossimina (E.G.O.), a.k.a. Suave

The Signature Series

Others who have finished all 10 drinks on this page have signed either this paper or the next page and dated it, in remembrance of family, good friends, great beverages and countless memories to which these drinks were made to salute. So when you enjoy all of these tasty beverages do so by thinking of all the good times we share. Sincerely Erik G. Ossimina (E.G.O.), a.k.a. Suave

The Signature Series

Sling Shot

Sling Shot

1 oz. Tangueray
1 oz. Christians Brothers Brandy
1 oz. Benedictine
1 oz. Dr. Mcgillicuddy's Cherry Schnapps
2 oz. Sprite
2 oz. Pineapple Juice
1 oz. Grenadine
9 - 1½ oz. Shot Glass
Spoon
Dash Bitters
Shaker
Ice

Put all ingredients into shaker and stir with spoon. Then strain shaker into the shot glasses and serve.

#81 A new variation of the sling is finally here! The Sling Shot is in good company with some already famous slings such as the Singapore Sling and the Strait Sling. You only need one shot to sign if you have 8 thirsty friends. So feel free to share or drink em all yourself!

Others who have finished this drink have signed either this paper or the previous page and dated it, in remembrance of family, good friends, great beverages and countless memories to which this drink was made to salute. So when you enjoy a Sling Shot do so by thinking of all the good times we share together. Sincerely Erik G. Ossimina (E.G.O.), a.k.a. Suave

Mist Maker

Mist Maker

¾ oz. Malibu Rum
¾ oz. Three Olives Cherry Vodka
1 Lipton Tea Bag
Water
12 oz. Coffee Mug

3 – 1 ½ oz Shot Glasses
Teapot
Dry Ice "Cubes"
Sugar
Spoon

*Do Not Touch or Put Dry Ice In Your Mouth
Read Instructions Provided On The Dry Ice Package For Proper Handling Procedures Then
Inform Everyone Involved

Your showmanship of the Mist Maker will make this drink truly MISTIFYING!

Boil enough water in the teapot to fill the coffee mug. While the water is boiling, it's your time to set the stage. When you make the Mist Maker do it with a little style and have everything ready to put on a good show for everyone that is there. Here is what you need to do:

Setting the Stage:

Fill one-shot glass with rum and one with the vodka. In the 3rd shot glass put dry ice cube(s), put these on the side for now along with sugar and the spoon. *(Beware the more ice the more mist but you will compromise the temperature of the drink and it will not be hot. The drink when enjoyed properly should at least be warm not cold.* Next put the tea bag into the coffee mug. Have everything ready in one spot where you're serving the drink. Preferably out of sight, but where you will be serving the drink. Now that the water has boiled you ready to begin.

Serving the Drink:

Pour boiling water into the coffee mug in front of patron. Then add the sugar, followed by the 2 shots of liquor. With a slide of hand empty the shot glass of dry ice into the mug and present it to the lucky soul that gets to enjoy the drink. Place a spoon on the side of cup with an empty shot glass so the consumer can remove the dry ice if they like. If you keep it in be careful while sipping the tea.

#82 Thru the mist it will all become clear. Tea for two will never be the same again. The Mist Maker is truly MISTIFYING! Keep children away from the dry ice at all times.

Others who have finished this drink have signed either this paper or the previous page and dated it, in remembrance of family, good friends, great beverages and countless memories to which this drink was made to salute. So when you enjoy The Mist Maker do so by thinking of all the good times we share together. Sincerely Erik G. Ossimina (E.G.O.), a.k.a. Suave

Creamy Apple Pie

Creamy Apple Pie

1 oz. Apple Barrel Schnapps
1 oz. Butterscotch Schnapps
5 oz. Heavy Cream
Cinnamon Powder
7 oz. Martini Glass
Shaker
Ice

Mix both of the schnapps along with the heavy cream and ice in a shaker. Strain into the martini glass and sprinkle a little cinnamon powder on top.

 # 83 An after dinner delight you and your guests will treasure time and time again. This will soon be an industry standard! Just like mom used to make. If you want to be daring, heat the schnapps in a microwave until warm then mix in shaker with the heavy cream deleting the ice cubes. Shake and strain into the martini glass. Finally put a small scoop of vanilla ice cream on top and make it Creamy Apple Pie Al La Mode.

Others who have finished this drink have signed either this paper or the previous page and dated it, in remembrance of family, good friends, great beverages and countless memories to which this drink was made to salute. So when you enjoy Creamy Apple Pie do so by thinking of all the good times we share together. Sincerely Erik G. Ossimina (E.G.O.), a.k.a. Suave

T K O

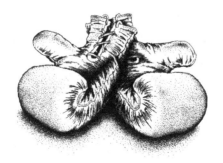

TKO

1 oz. Tangueray
1 oz. Ketel One
5 oz. Orange Juice
Shaker
Ice
7 oz. Martini Glass
Strainer

Pour all into shaker with ice. Shake for a few seconds. Let stand for a minute and then strain into martini glass.

#84 Watching the fights? Well why not pour yourself a Tko? Just be careful not to knock yourself out!

Others who have finished this drink have signed either this paper or the previous page and dated it, in remembrance of family, good friends, great beverages and countless memories to which this drink was made to salute. So when you enjoy a TKO do so by thinking of all the good times we share together. Sincerely Erik G. Ossimina (E.G.O.), a.k.a. Suave

Bitchen Banana

Bitchen Banana

2 oz. 99 Bananas

1 oz. Absolute Vodka

½ oz. Everclear

Banana

12 oz. Margarita Glass

Chocolate Syrup

Whipped Cream

Ice Crusher

Blender

Knife

Straw

1-Cup Milk

2 Scoops Vanilla Ice Cream

1-Cup Crushed Ice

Put liquor, ¾ of a banana, milk, ice cream and ice into blender. Blend until uniformly even. Using the remaining ¼ of banana as a garnish on the side of the glass. Splash chocolate syrup into margarita glass and on the banana, then fill glass with the mixture from the blender. Squirt whipped cream on one side of the glass next to the banana then top with more chocolate syrup. Add a straw and serve. Makes enough for 2.

 # 85 Hands down the toughest banana drink around. Whether hitting the waves or just strolling down the boardwalk the Bitchen Banana is sure to please. Feel free to dunk your banana into the drink. By the way I'm talking about the fruit sicko!

Others who have finished this drink have signed either this paper or the previous page and dated it, in remembrance of family, good friends, great beverages and countless memories to which this drink was made to salute. So when you enjoy a Bitchen Banana do so by thinking of all the good times we share together. Sincerely Erik G. Ossimina (E.G.O.), a.k.a. Suave

Stuck Up Bitch

Stuck Up Bitch

½ oz. Apple Barrel Schnapps
½ oz. Peach Tree Schnapps
3 oz. Smirnoff Passion Fruit Twist
1 oz. Grand Marnier
7 oz. Martini Glass
Shaker
Lemon
Cherry
Cocktail Sword
Straw
Ice

Pour liquor into shaker along with ice. Shake. Then stab cherry with the sword. Cut lemon a little less then in half. Using the smaller end of the lemon stab sword thru and place in the martini glass. Strain shaker into martini glass and serve.

#86 is shaken not stirred. The Stuck Up Bitch is made with the finest ingredients available. Make one today for that special someone. Perhaps you might even get them to let their hair down and relax a little.

Others who have finished this drink have signed either this paper or the previous page and dated it, in remembrance of family, good friends, great beverages and countless memories to which this drink was made to salute. So when you enjoy a Stuck Up Bitch do so by thinking of all the good times we share together. Sincerely Erik G. Ossimina (E.G.O.), a.k.a. Suave

The Comet

The Comet

½ oz.   **C** hristian Brothers Brandy
½ oz.   **O** ld Grand Dad
1   **M** ike's Hard Lemonade
½ oz.   **E** verclear
½ oz.   **T** riple Sec
Grenadine
12 oz. Rocks Glass
6 – 1½ oz. Shot Glasses
Shaker
Straw
Ice

Pour Liquor into shaker followed by ice. Then fill rocks glass halfway with ice. Stir shaker then strain into rocks glass. Top with a splash of Grenadine. Empty shaker into shot glasses and top each one with a splash of Grenadine. Serve the shot glasses with the drink, as they are the tail of the comet.

#87 The Comet is perfect to enjoy when friends, family and acquaintances are plentiful. Have the drink for yourself and pass out the shots to those around you. Sorry only those who have the drink can sign. But it's a great way to get others to try it. So explore the Cosmos by yourself or with others and you will see that Halley has nothing on my Comet!

Others who have finished this drink have signed either this paper or the previous page and dated it, in remembrance of family, good friends, great beverages and countless memories to which this drink was made to salute. So when you enjoy The Comet do so by thinking of all the good times we share together. Sincerely Erik G. Ossimina (E.G.O.), a.k.a. Suave

Tequila Tequila Tequila

Tequila Tequila Tequila

1 oz. Cabo Wabo Tequila

1 oz. Jose Cuervo Tequila

1 oz. Corazon Tequila

1-Cup Sour Mix

Pineapple Juice

Lime Juice

12 oz. Margarita Glass

Lime Wedge

3-5 Meal Worms

Ice Crusher

3 Cups Crushed Ice

Blender

Straw

Salt

Ice

In a blender mix the 3 oz. of tequila along with the sour mix and 2½ oz. of pineapple juice. Coat the rim of the margarita glass with limejuice then dip it in salt. Fill glass with crushed ice and empty blender into glass. Add a lime wedge and straw. Finally top drinks with a few mealworms.

#88 I came up with the name for this drink while thinking back to my honeymoon in Cancun, Mexico in 1998. Everywhere I went I would be asked if I wanted something to drink. I would reply," What do you have that's good?" The reply every time was Tequila, Tequila, Tequila! I have added some worms to this drink so that Mescal isn't the only one with a worm. So put 3-5 worms in your cocktail and enjoy. You don't have to eat the worms to sign, but I think you should :(eat em and smile:) It will turn any frown upside down. This drink really does eat like a meal! If you are really hungry feel free to add even more worms, I will not stop you.

Others who have finished this drink have signed either this paper or the previous page and dated it, in remembrance of family, good friends, great beverages and countless memories to which this drink was made to salute. So when you enjoy Tequila Tequila Tequila do so by thinking of all the good times we share together. Sincerely Erik G. Ossimina (E.G.O.), a.k.a. Suave

The GREEN Monster

The GREEN Monster

2 oz. Midori
2 oz. Bacardi
1 oz. Everclear
Rain lime Gatorade
Ice crusher
24 oz. Hurricane Glass
Dry Ice
Straw
2 Cups Crushed Ice

*Do Not Touch or Put Dry Ice In Your Mouth
Read Instructions Provided On The Dry Ice Package For Proper Handling Procedures Then
Inform Everyone Involved

Crush ice with ice crusher. Put crushed ice and drop 1 to 2 cubes of dry ice into the hurricane glass. Add liquor then Gatorade into the hurricane glass. The bubbling from the dry ice will mix the drink for you. Serve with a straw.

 # 89 is lurking about as it oozes this potent green liquid from its pores. Those who dare drink it are said to see clarity where there is only darkness, but others are doomed to turn into a monster themselves. So take heed and listen to my warning only thru the dark dismal corridor of your mind will you beat the monster within! Will you let the cold icy touch of the glass penetrate your soul?

Others who have finished this drink have signed either this paper or the previous page and dated it, in remembrance of family, good friends, great beverages and countless memories to which this drink was made to salute. So when you enjoy a Green Monster do so by thinking of all the good times we share together. Sincerely Erik G. Ossimina (E.G.O.), a.k.a. Suave

ChocoholicA

Chocoholic A

1 oz. Godiva
1 oz. Patron XO Café
4 oz. Heavy Cream
Shaker
Ice
7 oz. Martini Glass
Chocolate Syrup
Whipped Cream
Chocolate Kiss

Rim Martini glass with chocolate syrup and drop a little at the bottom of glass too. Then put liquor and heavy cream into the shaker along with some ice cubes. Next add 1 oz. of chocolate syrup into the shaker. Shake it up. Carefully strain into the martini glass. Spray some whipped cream on top of drink and splash with a little chocolate syrup. Finally place chocolate kiss on top.

#90 Here's the dreams that you've been after. I promise you no lies. Laughter, laughter all you'll hear and see is laughter. Laughter, laughter. Laughing till you cry. ChocoholicA is like nothing you have ever seen or tasted before! So crank up the Gods of Metal and enjoy one today! So if you don't already have Master of Puppets by Metallica I suggest you go out and get it. In my opinion it's one of the best!

Others who have finished this drink have signed either this paper or the previous page and dated it, in remembrance of family, good friends, great beverages and countless memories to which this drink was made to salute. So when you enjoy ChocoholicA do so by thinking of all the good times we share together. Sincerely Erik G. Ossimina (E.G.O.), a.k.a. Suave

The Signature Series

Others who have finished all 10 drinks on this page have signed either this paper or the next page and dated it, in remembrance of family, good friends, great beverages and countless memories to which these drinks were made to salute. So when you enjoy all of these tasty beverages do so by thinking of all the good times we share. Sincerely Erik G. Ossimina (E.G.O.), a.k.a. Suave

The Signature Series

A Poisonous Apple

"And can you absolutely guarantee
that these apples are poisonous?"

A Poisonous Apple

3 oz. Sour Apple Schnapps
1 oz. Crystal Head Vodka
1 oz. Bacardi 151
7 oz. Martini Glass
Shaker
Ice

Mix all in a shaker with ice then strain into the martini glass and serve.

 # 91 Dying for a tasty beverage, well wait no longer!

Others who have finished this drink have signed either this paper or the previous page and dated it, in remembrance of family, good friends, great beverages and countless memories to which this drink was made to salute. So when you enjoy A Poisonous Apple do so by thinking of all the good times we share together. Sincerely Erik G. Ossimina (E.G.O.), a.k.a. Suave

Nuclear Assault

Nuclear Assault

1 oz. Everclear
2 oz. Malibu
Kool Aid Tropical Punch
Sprite
Crack Ups (popping candy)
16 oz. Pint Glass
Shaker
Straw
Ice

Fill shaker ½ way with ice. Pour alcohol into shaker along with the Tropical Punch. Shake and then pour into pint glass. Top with Sprite. Empty a packet of Crack Ups into the drink and serve.

#92 when you wake up and your mouth asks what happened just tell yourself that you survived a Nuclear Assault; no further explanation will be necessary.

Others who have finished this drink have signed either this paper or the previous page and dated it, in remembrance of family, good friends, great beverages and countless memories to which this drink was made to salute. So when you enjoy a Nuclear Assault do so by thinking of all the good times we share together. Sincerely Erik G. Ossimina (E.G.O.), a.k.a. Suave

The Iridescent Rainbow

The Iridescent Rainbow

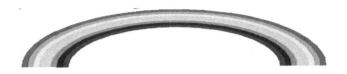

¼ Cup Midori Melon

¼ Cup Absolute Citron

¼ Cup Strawberry Leroux

¼ Cup Grand Marnier

¼ Cup Blue Curacao

¼ Cup Grape Pucker

8 oz. Clear Plastic Cups

Whipped Cream

Green Jell-O

Yellow Jell-O

Red Jell-O

Orange Jell-O

Blue Jell-O

Purple Jell-O

Water

Rainbow Sprinkles

The liquor above goes with the Jell-O to the right of it. Start with the green, then yellow, red, orange, blue and finally top with purple. Use a whole packet of Jell-O for each layer. One-cup hot water, ¾ cup cold water and ¼ cup of liquor. Do one color at a time. Before adding the next layer make sure the previous layer has cooled. Right before serving top with whipped cream and Rainbow sprinkles. ☺

 # 93 Wash away the clouds with The Iridescent Rainbow! This will bring a smile to all the girls' faces that indulge in this treat. Not as strong as the original Rainbow, this one will let you simply sit back and savor the flavor of colors brought before you. Enjoy!

Others who have finished this drink have signed either this paper or the previous page and dated it, in remembrance of family, good friends, great beverages and countless memories to which this drink was made to salute. So when you enjoy The Iridescent Rainbow do so by thinking of all the good times we share together. Sincerely Erik G. Ossimina (E.G.O.), a.k.a. Suave

Simply Sour

Simply Sour

½ oz. Absolute Citron
½ oz. Peach Schnapps
½ oz. Apple Schnapps
Lemon
Lime
Grater
Lime Juice
Shaker
1 ½ oz. Shot Glass
Ice

Pour liquor into shaker with ice and shake until shaker gets icy. Strain into shot glass and top with limejuice. Shave lemon & lime peel with a fine grater. Layer citrus shavings on top of drink as garnish.

#94 Pucker up! I hope you have no cuts on your lips it might sting a little. So why not go out and give someone a kiss after trying this one.

Others who have finished this drink have signed either this paper or the previous page and dated it, in remembrance of family, good friends, great beverages and countless memories to which this drink was made to salute. So when you enjoy Simply Sour do so by thinking of all the good times we share together. Sincerely Erik G. Ossimina (E.G.O.), a.k.a. Suave

Toxic Tonic

Toxic Tonic

1 oz. Bombay Sapphire
1 oz. Crystal Head Vodka
½ oz. Everclear
Tonic Water
12 oz. Rocks Glass
2 Sip Straws

Ice
Cucumber
Knife
Lemon Juice
Lime Juice

Fill rocks glass with ice. Give a generous squirt of lemon and limejuice. Then pour gin, vodka and Everclear into glass. Fill with tonic. Then give another generous squirt of lemon and limejuice. Next cut two cucumber slices into ¼ thick wheels. Cut wheels in half and place on rim of glass in a fan like fashion. Serve with 2 bar straws.

#95 I think the skull and cross bones says it all! You might just need the cucumber fan to cool off afterwards I thought, but to my amazement this drink was so refreshing that I was taken back with sheer delight. I really don't like tonic but to my surprise everything mixed so well together that I didn't want to stop drinking the Toxic Tonic and had to have one more you will too☺

Others who have finished this drink have signed either this paper or the previous page and dated it, in remembrance of family, good friends, great beverages and countless memories to which this drink was made to salute. So when you enjoy Toxic Tonic do so by thinking of all the good times we share together. Sincerely Erik G. Ossimina (E.G.O.), a.k.a. Suave

Magnificent Margarita

Are You Magnificent?

Magnificent Margarita

4 oz. Jose Cuervo Tequila
2 oz. Strawberry Leroux
2 oz. Absolute Vodka
2 Cups of Mr. & Mrs. T Strawberry Daiquiri Margarita Mix
1 Cup Orange Juice
Sugar
12 oz. Margarita Glasses
Orange Wheel
Strawberry
Blender
3 Cups Crushed Ice
Whipped Cream
Ice Crusher

Coat outer edge of margarita glass with orange juice (I just use the orange wheel to go around outer edge of glass) then cover edge of glass with sugar. Pour alcohol into blender along with the margarita mix and orange juice. Fill blender with crushed ice. Blend thoroughly. Pour into margarita glasses and garnish with a sliced strawberry and orange wheel. Spray whipped cream on half of the drink and on top of strawberry. Makes 4 drinks.

 # 96 A crown jewel in the margarita lineup. The Magnificent Margarita will sparkle like a diamond in the rough! A great drink to break out when friends stop. Bang! 1.2..3... you're done and you have 4 tasty drinks to serve in no time at all.

Others who have finished this drink have signed either this paper or the previous page and dated it, in remembrance of family, good friends, great beverages and countless memories to which this drink was made to salute. So when you enjoy a Magnificent Margarita do so by thinking of all the good times we share together. Sincerely Erik G. Ossimina (E.G.O.), a.k.a. Suave

Hot Shot

CAUTION
Risk
of fire

Hot Shot

1 oz. Grande Absinthe
½ oz. Amaretto
1 ½ oz. Shot Glass
Glass Coaster
Lighter
Spoon

Pour Amaretto into a shot glass. Using a spoon float Grande Absinthe into shot glass. (When using the spoon to float the mixture, turn the spoon upside down). Light and serve. (Put out flame before drinking!) Use a glass coaster to place on top of shot glass to extinguish the flame or something non-flammable.

#97 Amaze your friends, dazzle onlookers and keep firefighters working. Just kidding but be careful just the same when igniting drinks. This one is served best when accompanied by a bunch of shots. So get the gang together and light up the night! As with all lit drinks make sure to have a working fire extinguisher at the ready. Keep all other flammable things away from the area that you will be working in as well. Remember have fun, but be safe.

Others who have finished this drink have signed either this paper or the previous page and dated it, in remembrance of family, good friends, great beverages and countless memories to which this drink was made to salute. So when you enjoy a Hot Shot do so by thinking of all the good times we share together. Sincerely Erik G. Ossimina (E.G.O.), a.k.a. Suave

Fire & Ice

Fire & Ice

2 oz. Absolute Vodka
2 oz. Ketel One Vodka
1-Cup Fruit Punch
1-Cup Cool Blue Gatorade
6 Cups Crushed Ice
Ice Crusher
Blender
2 – 24 oz. Hurricane Glasses
Spoon
Straw

Crush 6 cups of crushed ice using the ice crusher. Take 3 cups of the crushed ice and put in blender with Ketel One Vodka and the Gatorade. Blend until thick and fill each hurricane glass half way. Wash out the blender and add the rest of the crushed ice along with the Absolute Vodka and the fruit punch. Blend until thick and pour gently over a spoon into the hurricane glasses and serve with a straw.

#98 Fire & Ice will run through your veins after every delightful sip. Drink them separately or stir them together. You'll be a winner whichever way you choose. Make a bunch today and sign below! You can even do a bunch of layers if you choose. This drink is truly refreshing and perfect on a hot summers day or a chilly winters night! Watch out for a brain freeze!

Others who have finished this drink have signed either this paper or the previous page and dated it, in remembrance of family, good friends, great beverages and countless memories to which this drink was made to salute. So when you enjoy Fire & Ice do so by thinking of all the good times we share together. Sincerely Erik G. Ossimina (E.G.O.), a.k.a. Suave

Bottle Rocket

Bottle Rocket

1 Budweiser Beer Bottle
½ oz. Southern Comfort
½ oz. Bacardi
1½ oz. Shot Glasse

Pour both liquors into shot glass then empty into the beer bottle. Tap on the top of the beer bottle with another beer bottle and watch it explode. If you don't want to tap the bottle then put your thumb over the bottle and turn bottle upside down then right side up.

#99 A great drink with friends but best kept outdoors especially when tapping on the beer. Watch out for chipping or breaking of the bottle. If this occurs just simply throw out bottle and start over. While I recommend Budweiser for the beer, feel free to chose your own favorite. My neighbor Rick and sister were the first ones to slam this one down. So why not join the in the celebration known as life and drink up and sign below! You too can blast off and reach for the stars.

Others who have finished this drink have signed either this paper or the previous page and dated it, in remembrance of family, good friends, great beverages and countless memories to which this drink was made to salute. So when you enjoy Bottle Rocket do so by thinking of all the good times we share together. Sincerely Erik G. Ossimina (E.G.O.), a.k.a. Suave

Jack Ass

Jack Ass

1 oz. **J**ack Daniels
1 oz. **A**maretto
1 oz. **S**outhern Comfort
1 oz. **S**loe Gin
Shaker
Ice
4 - 1½ oz. Shot glasses (enough glasses for the amount of people playing)

Put ice in shaker followed by the liquor. Strain shaker equally into shot glasses after chilled. Serve. This Makes 4 one oz. shots enough for 4 people to do one round.

#100 the last beverage in my crazy assortment of drinks has finally arrived. 1 shot to sign is all it takes. But to make it interesting I made it into a drinking game. Each player takes a loaded shot glass and all together count out loud to 5. When you reach 5, drink shot and slam shot glass down on table. Last one with an empty shot glass on the table loses and has to make or buy the next round. The first one to give up is the Jackass! Have fun and play nice.

Congratulations if with this drink you have completed the Signature Series. I hope that you have enjoyed them all and will continue to enjoy them for the years to come. I salute you!

Others who have finished this drink have signed either this paper or the previous page and dated it, in remembrance of family, good friends, great beverages and countless memories to which this drink was made to salute. So when you enjoy a Jack Ass do so by thinking of all the good times we share together. Sincerely Erik G. Ossimina (E.G.O.), a.k.a. Suave

Signature Series Non-Alcoholic Recipes

- **Non-Alcoholic Twist**

- **Ossimina's Hot Non-Alcoholic Cider**

- **Non-Alcoholic Cherry Bomb**

- **Non-Alcoholic Sugary Strawberry**

- **Non-Alcoholic Orange Dream**

- **Saints & Sinners Non-Alcoholic Punch**

- **Non-Alcoholic Rainbow**

- **Razzle Dazzle**

Non-Alcoholic Twist

½ Cup Milk
3 Scoops Butterfinger Ice Cream
3 Cups Crushed Ice
Chocolate Syrup
Butterscotch Syrup
Whipped Cream
24 oz. Hurricane Glass
Ice Crusher
Blender
Straw

Crush ice using the ice crusher then put in blender with milk and ice cream. Blend till mixture is smooth. Drizzle chocolate and butterscotch syrup in the hurricane glass. Then fill glass with the mixture from the blender. Spray whipped cream on top of glass and drizzle the syrups on top. Serve with a straw.

This is one of eight non-alcoholic drinks for those who for whatever reason cannot enjoy one of my alcoholic signature drinks.

A non-alcoholic treat the whole family can enjoy!

Ossimina's Hot Non-Alcoholic Cider

Apple Cider
1/3-Cup Brown Sugar
Cinnamon Sticks
Saucepan
Apple
Orange
Coffee Mug
Cheesecloth
String

Cut apples and oranges into thin slices. Put them into cheesecloth. Add some cinnamon sticks and tie up with string. In a saucepan, add cider and sugar. Put cheesecloth in the saucepan and bring to a boil. Reduce heat, cover and let simmer for 10 minutes. Discard cheesecloth and pour contents of saucepan into the coffee mugs. Garnish with cinnamon stick, stir and serve.

This is the second of eight non-alcoholic drinks for those who for whatever reason cannot enjoy one of my alcoholic signature drinks.

A non-alcoholic treat the whole family can enjoy!

Non-Alcoholic Cherry Bomb

Cherries
Milk
Chocolate (Melting Chocolate)
Medicine Dropper
Double Boiler
Beater
Serving Plate or Platter
Aluminum Foil
Cookie Sheet
Chocolate Syrup
Knife

Melt chocolate in a double boiler. Next dip (dry) cherries into chocolate and place on a foil lined cookie sheet. Let cool. When chocolate has hardened cut a small hole on the top of the cherry with a knife. Then using the end of the beater punch a hole into the cherry. (I find the small end of the beater makes a great puncture hole in the cherry; you can use anything handy to make the hole a little larger for the alcohol to sit in). In a cup mix chocolate syrup and milk. Then fill medicine dropper with the chocolate milk and inject into the top of cherries. Drizzle chocolate syrup on platter and serve.

This is the third of eight non-alcoholic drinks for those who for whatever reason cannot enjoy one of my alcoholic signature drinks.

A non-alcoholic treat the whole family can enjoy!

Non-Alcoholic Sugared Strawberry

Strawberry
Sugar
Strawberry Jelly
Serving Plate or Platter
Shot Glass
Knife

Hollow out a large strawberry with a knife. Next roll strawberry around in a bowl of sugar. Put strawberry jelly into the strawberry. Place in a shot glass and serve!

This is the fourth of eight non-alcoholic drinks for those who for whatever reason cannot enjoy one of my alcoholic signature drinks.

A non-alcoholic treat the whole family can enjoy!

Non-Alcoholic
Orange Dream

2 Scoops Orange Sherbet
1 Bottle Stewarts Orange and Cream
Whipped Cream
Orange Wheel
Cherry
Straw
Frozen 16 oz. Pint Glass
Blender
Crushed Ice
Ice Crusher

Blend sherbet, Stewarts Orange and Cream and crushed ice together in a blender. (Keep top of blender loose and allow gas to escape when blending). Pour into a frozen pint glass & top with whipped cream. Garnish the drink with a cherry and orange wheel. Serve with a straw.

This is the fifth of eight non-alcoholic drinks for those who for whatever reason cannot enjoy one of my alcoholic signature drinks.

A non-alcoholic treat the whole family can enjoy!

Saint's & Sinner's Non-Alcoholic Punch

6 oz. Pineapple Juice
2 Cups Orange Juice
2 Cups Cranberry Juice
¼ Tablespoons of Sugar
12 oz. Sprite
Beer Pitcher
12 oz. Rocks Glass
Orange
Strawberries
Raspberries
Lemon
Lime
Ice

Fill pitcher halfway with ice. Put sugar into the pitcher followed with pineapple juice, orange juice, cranberry juice and Sprite. Stir. Cut a lemon, lime and orange into a wheel and then into fours. Also slice strawberries and raspberries into chunks and put into pitcher. Serve in rocks glasses full of ice. Add 2 small bar straws. Keep pitcher refrigerated when not serving.

This is the sixth of eight non-alcoholic drinks for those who for whatever reason cannot enjoy one of my alcoholic signature drinks.

A non-alcoholic treat the whole family can enjoy!

Non-Alcoholic Rainbow

Green Jell-O
Yellow Jell-O
Red Jell-O
Orange Jell-O
Blue Jell-O
Purple Jell-O
8 oz. Clear Plastic Cups
Water
Whipped Cream
Rainbow Sprinkles

Start with the green, then yellow, red, orange, blue and finally top with purple. Use a whole packet of Jell-O for each layer using one-cup Hot water and 1 cup cold water for each packet. Do one color at a time. Before adding the next layer make sure the previous layer has cooled. Right before serving top with whipped cream and Rainbow sprinkles. ☺

This is the seven of eight non-alcoholic drinks for those who for whatever reason cannot enjoy one of my alcoholic signature drinks.

A non-alcoholic treat the whole family can enjoy!

Razzle Dazzle

Orange Juice
Pineapple Juice
Mr. & Mrs. T's Strawberry Daiquiri Margarita Mix
24 oz. Hurricane Glass
Cranbury Juice
Straw
Umbrella
Orange Wheel
Lemon Wedge
Lime Wedge
Cherry
Shaker
Ice

Put ice, juices and daiquiri mix into shaker and shake it up. Present your drink in a razzle-dazzle fashion using the garnishes, umbrella and straw. If you feel the need to add another garnish to razzle it up even more, I give you creative license to go crazy. Make whoever is drinking the Razzle Dazzle feel that way☺.

This is the eighth of eight non-alcoholic drinks for those who for whatever reason cannot enjoy one of my alcoholic signature drinks.

A non-alcoholic treat the whole family can enjoy!

(Your own Signature Drink)

Ingredients:

Directions:

A Little Something:

(Your own Signature Drink)

Ingredients:

Directions:

A Little Something:

_____

(Your own Signature Drink)

Ingredients:

Directions:

A Little Something:

_____

(Your own Signature Drink)

Ingredients:

Directions:

A Little Something:

_____

(Your own Signature Drink)

Ingredients:

Directions:

A Little Something:

_____

(Your own Signature Drink)

Ingredients:

Directions:

A Little Something:

(Your own Signature Drink)

Ingredients:

Directions:

A Little Something:

(Your own Signature Drink)

Ingredients:

Directions:

A Little Something:

(Your own Signature Drink)

Ingredients:

Directions:

A Little Something:

(Your own Signature Drink)

Ingredients:

Directions:

A Little Something:

_____

(Your own Signature Drink)

Ingredients:

Directions:

A Little Something:

The Signature Series II

Looking to feature the craziest drinks from around the world in my upcoming book The Signature Series II. Do you have what it takes to make the cut? Submit your drink and we will find out! Include:

* **Drink Name**
* **Ingredients**
* **Instructions On Making Your Drink**
* **A Little Something About You & Your Drink**
* **Photo Of You and Your Drink**

Send To: TSSdrinksubmissions@yahoo.com

Flying High
Above the
Rest!

VISIONARY

252

This page was intentionally left blank until I decided to let you know that I intentionally left it blank thereby compromising the blankness of the page. Now the page is in fact not blank at all. Just the ramblings of a mad man lurk here. So feel free to use this page for whatever you like. Perhaps you might put a slash on this page for each time someone has had one of the drinks in this book. Or you might use this page for writing down some of your favorite drinks, but then it will probably just be a copy of pages 11 to 14. Why not come up with something different. Let me know what you come up with. Maybe you will take whiteout and truly make this page blank. Send me a picture and explanation of what you did and I might post it on one of my pages, lets see who is the most creative!

For this and other available merchandise please visit me @

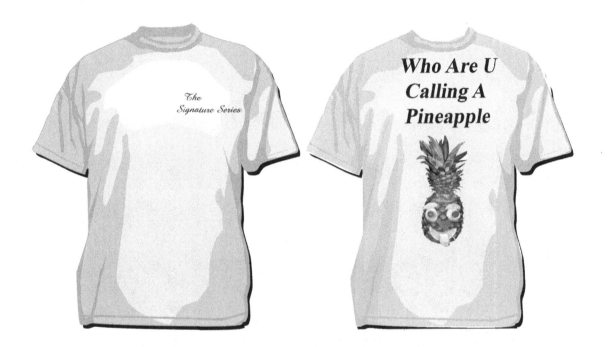

www.TheSignatureSeriesbyEgo.com

Myspace: The Signature Series
www.myspace.com/The-Signature-Series
Facebook: The Signature Series